This book is to be returned on or before the last date stamped below.

OXFORD CHILDREN'S REFERENCE LIBRARY

AFRICA

OXFORD CHILDREN'S REFERENCE LIBRARY
General Editors: Patrick Moore and Laura E. Salt
Illustrations Editors: Helen Mary Petter and Laura Cohn

1
THE UNIVERSE
By Colin Ronan
Illustrated by David A. Hardy

2
EXPLORING THE WORLD
By Patrick Moore
Illustrated by Joan Williams and Clifford Bayly

3
ANIMALS
By Maurice Burton
Illustrated by Edward Osmond

4
INDIA AND HER NEIGHBOURS
By Taya Zinkin
Illustrated by Biman Mullick

5
STORIES OF COURAGE
By Cleodie Mackinnon
Illustrated by Peter Branfield

6
THE EARTH
By Jean Petrie
Illustrated by David A. Hardy

7
RUSSIA AND HER NEIGHBOURS
By Lovett F. Edwards
Illustrated by Clifford Bayly

8
MORE ANIMALS
By Maurice Burton
Illustrated by Sheila Hawkins and others

9
STORIES TOLD ROUND THE WORLD
By Taya Zinkin
Illustrated by Graham Oakley

10
AFRICA
By Arnold Curtis
Illustrated by Caroline Sassoon

11
A BOOK OF SCIENCE
By Colin Ronan
Illustrated by Peter North

12
THE ANCIENT WORLD
By Robert Ogilvie
Illustrated by Graham Oakley

13
THE ARAB WORLD
By Sheila Kaye
Illustrated by Ulrica Lloyd

14
STORIES OF GREAT LEADERS
By Cleodie Mackinnon

Oxford Children's Reference Library

10

AFRICA

by
ARNOLD CURTIS

illustrated by
CAROLINE SASSOON

TOLLINGTON PARK
SCHOOL,
TURLE ROAD, N.4.

OXFORD UNIVERSITY PRESS
1969

Oxford University Press, Ely House, London W.1

GLASGOW NEW YORK TORONTO MELBOURNE WELLINGTON
CAPE TOWN SALISBURY IBADAN NAIROBI LUSAKA ADDIS ABABA
BOMBAY CALCUTTA MADRAS KARACHI LAHORE DACCA
KUALA LUMPUR HONG KONG TOKYO

© *Oxford University Press 1969*

036529

916

TOLLINGTON PARK
SCHOOL,
TURLE ROAD, N.4.

PRINTED IN GREAT BRITAIN BY JESSE BROAD & CO. LTD.

CONTENTS

		Page
	INTRODUCTION	6
1	DARKEST AFRICA	8
2	THE CONTINENT OF AFRICA	10
3	THE PEOPLES OF AFRICA	12
4	THE NILE VALLEY	14
5	THE KINGDOM OF KUSH	16
6	THE KINGDOM OF AXUM	18
7	SOME AFRICAN BIRDS	20
8	THE SAHARA DESERT	22
9	THE KINGDOM OF GHANA	24
10	TIMBUKTU	26
11	ALONG THE RIVER NIGER	28
12	THE TUG-OF-WAR	30
13	THE PORTUGUESE IN WEST AFRICA	32
14	THE SLAVE TRADE IN WEST AFRICA	34
15	MARY KINGSLEY TRAVELS IN WEST AFRICA	36
16	SENEGAL	38
17	DR. AGGREY THE SCHOOLMASTER	40
18	COCOA FARMING IN GHANA	42
19	THE TALKING DRUMS OF THE CONGO	44
20	THE BUSHMEN OF THE KALAHARI DESERT	46
21	CHAKA AND THE ZULUS	48
22	PAUL KRUGER AND THE AFRIKANERS	50
23	CECIL RHODES	52
24	SOUTH AFRICAN FRUIT FARMING	54
25	JOHANNESBURG	56
26	THE EUROPEANS IN AFRICA	58
27	TSETSE FLIES OF TROPICAL AFRICA	60
28	ZIMBABWE	62
29	THE ZAMBEZI RIVER	64
30	THE HARE AND THE PUMPKINS	66
31	KILWA	68
32	IVORY AND SLAVES IN EAST AFRICA	70

33	THE MAN-EATERS OF TSAVO	72
34	THE KINGDOM OF BUGANDA	74
35	THE HYENAS AND THEIR MEDICINE-MAN	76
36	A GAME PARK	78
37	THE MOUNTAINS OF EAST AFRICA	80
38	THE RIFT VALLEY AND THE GREAT LAKES	82
39	THE MASAI	84
40	A KIKUYU VILLAGE IN KENYA	86
41	A SOMALI ENCAMPMENT	88
42	LOCUSTS IN THE HORN OF AFRICA	90
43	ETHIOPIA	92
	INDEX	94

INTRODUCTION

THIS BOOK, like some others in the *Oxford Children's Reference Library*, is concerned with drawing a picture of an area of the world, in this case the continent of Africa. It gives something of the history of this great continent; it describes its main geographical features — its great rivers and lakes, mountains and forests, grasslands and deserts; and it gives an account of its many different peoples, the life they live, and the crops they grow. It tells of their customs, their various languages, and the folk-tales which they tell round the fire in the evening. It also describes some of the many birds and animals in which Africa is so rich.

This book is principally concerned with Africa south of the Sahara Desert — the land of the Negroes and related peoples. The Arab people of North Africa are described in another book in this series, Book 13. But there is mention of the Egyptian civilizations of the Nile Valley because their influence spread up the Nile, especially to the people of Ethiopia and the Sudan. The story of Africa is carried from the Nile across the desert to Timbuktu and the ancient kingdoms of Ghana and Benin. It continues down the west coast, round South Africa, and up through the countries of East Africa, until it reaches Ethiopia and the Nile again. Accounts of the great rivers and lakes carry the story inland.

Africa is an old country and also a very new one. In ancient days, when Europeans knew very little about the 'Dark Continent', there were great African empires, such as Axum and Zimbabwe, the history of which is now being rediscovered. Then, for hundreds of years, traders came from Europe in search of gold, ivory, and slaves, missionaries explored further inland, and settlers followed, seeking farmlands. Gradually the whole continent was opened up and parcelled out among the European nations — mainly Britain, Holland, France, Portugal and Belgium. During recent years, one by one, the African peoples are winning back their homelands and are building up their own independent nations. They have to change quickly from tribal peoples to nations able to take their place in a modern world, and they have many difficulties to face, as all young countries have. But their future is full of hope.

1 DARKEST AFRICA

Deep in the African tropical forest

IN THE STORY of mankind different parts of the world have been particularly important at different times. There was a time when the Chinese were more advanced than any other peoples. Later, the Greeks were the leaders of the world, and then the Romans built their great empire. In more recent times, the countries of western Europe carried their ideas and way of life all over the world, building new civilizations in America and elsewhere.

Africa, the second largest of the continents (see Map, p. 11), often appears to the rest of the world to be very old and very backward. Europeans used to speak of it as the 'Dark Continent'. The skins of most of its people were dark; it was dark inside a tropical forest; and there were stories of such dark doings as human sacrifice and witchcraft. But what the people of Europe really meant when they called Africa 'dark' was that they knew very little about what went on there. In fact, there have been at least two periods when what happened in Africa was extremely important to the world.

The first period is right at the beginning of the human race. We know that, when living things had been developing on our Earth for millions of years, a creature appeared with hands and feet which could grip things. This creature was the ancestor of monkeys, apes, and early man. Nature made all kinds of experiments before arriving at the kind of man we know today, and some of the most interesting of these experiments took place in Africa. Many important remains of early man-type creatures have been dug up by scientists in eastern and southern Africa, especially in the central part of East Africa. If we think of the story of the Garden of Eden, there is no more suitable place for us to imagine it than in the Great Rift Valley, near the border between Kenya and Tanzania (see Chapter 38).

The second period when Africa was important to the world was between about 3,000 B.C. and 1,000 B.C., when ancient Egypt under the Pharaohs was at her greatest. The system of living securely together in organized groups, where every man has his own special work to do, is what we call civilization. It began in the Middle East in river valleys, where farming was easy and people could grow more than they needed for themselves and their families. It developed in the valley of the Nile in Egypt (see Chapter 4), and spread along the countries of the Mediterranean. It also spread south, up the Nile valley, and helped to shape the history of the interior of Africa.

But, although ideas and ways of farming spread from Egypt southwards, Egypt's great discovery of writing did not spread further south than Ethiopia. And so, for most of Africa south of the Sahara Desert, there was no history written at all until about 100 years ago, when Europeans began exploring Africa. For all the thousands of years before this, the history has to be built up from legends and stories in people's memories and from the things which have survived from the past, and which have been dug up by archaeologists (people who study the past). So the history of much of Africa is still being discovered and pieced together, whereas that of Europe was written down almost as it happened.

The north coast of Africa was always well known to Europeans. But south of that lay the great desert across which it was difficult to travel (see Chapter 8). The rest of Africa's coast was unfriendly (see Chapter 2), and the inland

A gorge in the Rift Valley

was hot and difficult to travel in. So Europeans tried to break into Africa only when they wanted something — gold, precious stones, ivory, or slaves. The Romans went there to get ostrich feathers and wild animals for the gladiators to fight. 'There is always something new from Africa,' they used to say. Otherwise Africa remained unknown to the people of Europe.

Africa still has many things the rest of the world wants — gold, diamonds, groundnuts, coffee, cocoa, and plenty of others; but today people buy them instead of taking them. With the money, Africans can buy the manufactured goods and machines they need. There are about fifty small nations in Africa now, most of them very young, who want to develop as quickly as they can their own kind of modern way of life within the world family of nations. Africa is no longer a Dark Continent. She is on her way up once more, and she is full of vigorous, determined people who mean to reach the heights, even if they make many mistakes in doing so.

What one of the first men in Africa might have looked like.

2 THE CONTINENT OF AFRICA

IF YOU LOOK at this map of Africa from the side, you can easily imagine that it is shaped like the head of one of its own great animals — a rhinoceros. Under its neck lies the South Atlantic Ocean. At the back of its head is the Mediterranean. The Red Sea lies behind its horn; while the horn itself juts out into the Indian Ocean. South Africa is the nose. Its eye, Lake Victoria, the second largest lake in the world, seems to be peering towards the South Pole.

It is only within the last 100 years that Europe and Africa have come to know each other at all well. If we look at the geography of Africa we can see good reasons why the rest of the world took so long to discover it. Across the north of the continent the Sahara Desert stretches for 3,000 miles, cutting Europe off from the rest of Africa. Bartholomew Diaz sailed right down the West African coast from Portugal in 1487, and very shortly after, Vasco da Gama sailed right round Africa to reach India. But little tempted the sailors to land, for the coasts were blocked by reefs or sandbanks and battered by great ocean waves, and ships could not sail up the rivers because of swampy deltas on the coasts and rapids and cataracts inland. So, apart from some trading settlements on the coast, Europeans did not really explore Africa until the 19th century.

Most of Africa was thinly populated, and what people there were seem to have been continually on the move. The soil over much of the country is poor and easily exhausted, so the people farmed by what we call 'shifting cultivation' — that is, they cultivated a piece of ground for a while until they had used up its goodness, and then they moved on to new land. With this kind of farming it takes a great deal of land to provide food for comparatively few people. So the population did not increase. Today, as we shall see, this situation is changing fast.

In this book we are mainly concerned with Africa south of the Sahara Desert, which cuts the Mediterranean lands off from the rest of Africa. We will be moving from the great Nile valley in the north-east, across the desert and the grasslands of the Sudan, to the river Niger and the countries of West Africa. We will travel southwards to the basin of the river Congo and on over the Kalahari Desert to South Africa, where the Dutch and the British made their first settlements. We shall come up through the lovely mountainous country of East Africa, over the Zambesi river, by the great lakes of the Rift valley, until we reach the source of the river Nile. We shall end in the horn of Africa and the kingdom of Ethiopia.

KEY TO MAP

1 EGYPT
2 LIBYA
3 TUNISIA
4 ALGERIA
5 MOROCCO
6 MAURITANIA
7 SENEGAL
8 GAMBIA
9 GUINEA
10 SIERRA LEONE
11 LIBERIA
12 IVORY COAST
13 MALI
14 VOLTA
15 GHANA
16 TOGO
17 DAHOMEY
18 NIGER
19 NIGERIA
20 CHAD
21 CENTRAL AFRICAN REP.
22 CAMEROON
23 CONGO BRAZZAVILLE
24 CONGO KINSHASA
25 ANGOLA
26 ZAMBIA
27 BOTSWANA
28 SOUTH AFRICA
29 RHODESIA
30 MOZAMBIQUE
31 MALAWI
32 TANZANIA
33 KENYA
34 UGANDA
35 SOMALI
36 SUDAN
37 ETHIOPIA

The countries of Africa today

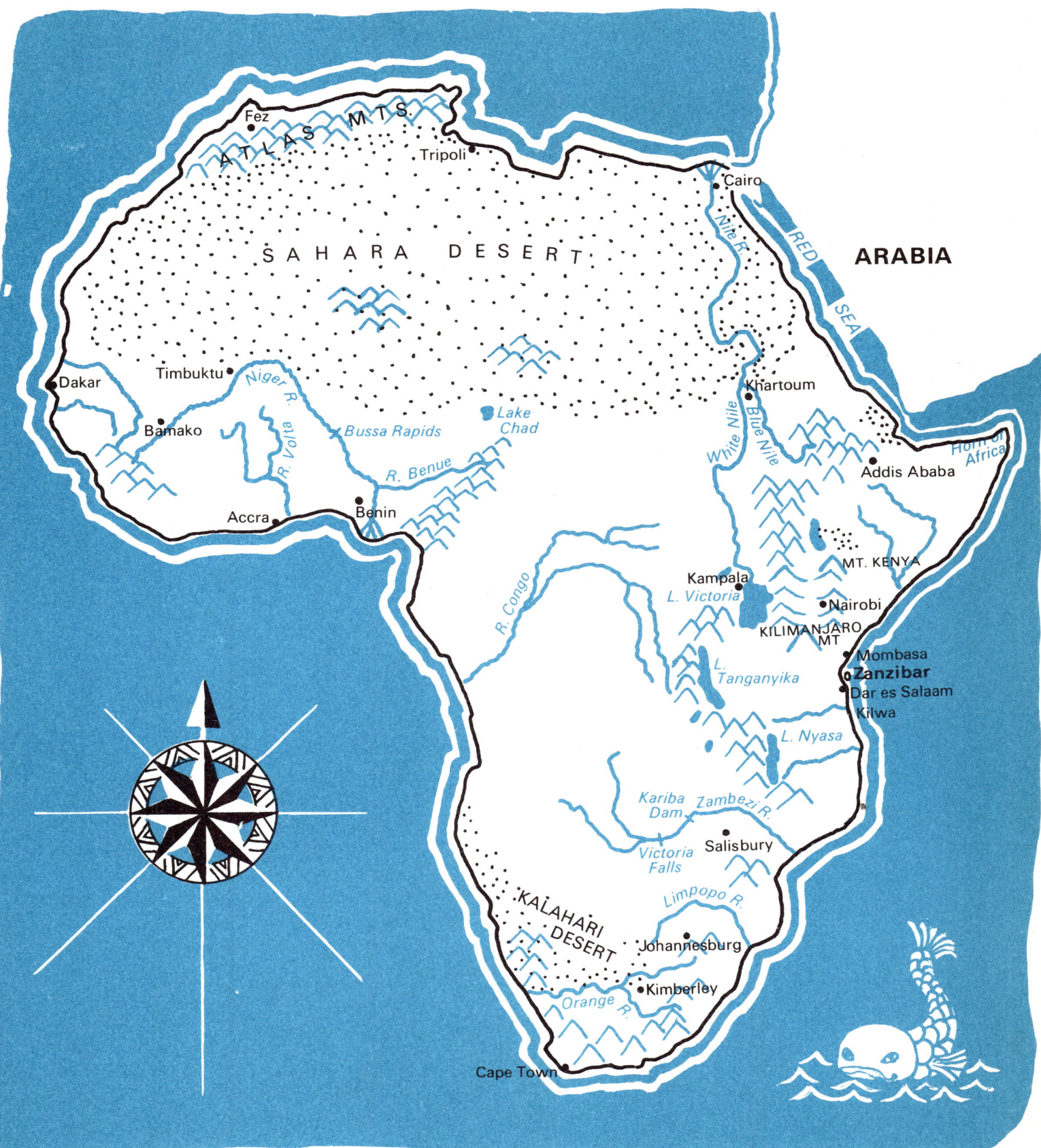

3 THE PEOPLES OF AFRICA

A Pygmy family in the Congo Forest

WHAT SORT OF people are the Africans? This is never an easy question to answer, because people have become very mixed up over the centuries, and there is now no such thing as a pure 'race'. The people of the fifty or so countries of Africa include men with black skins, brown skins, white skins, and even yellow skins. We can, however, roughly group the people who have been living in Africa since before history began into five groups — the Bushmen, the Pygmies, the Hottentots, the Negroes, and the lighter-skinned people who live mainly in the north and north-east, and are not very different from the people of southern Europe. They mostly have light-brown skins, noses which tend to be long rather than flat, and wavy hair. The people of ancient Egypt were like this.

Negroid peoples now occupy most of Africa south of the Sahara Desert. Most have dark skins, some much darker than others, and some almost black. Their lips turn outwards, and their noses tend to be flat rather than long. They usually have woolly black hair. They are quite tall, and for their height they are usually slender.

The Bushmen and the Pygmies are what are left of the old hunting and food-gathering peoples who once roamed over a great part of the continent. They have gradually been pushed into those parts of the country which are not suitable for farming. The Bushmen live in the deserts in the western part of the Republic of South Africa (see Chapter 20), and the Pygmies live in the depths of the Congo forests. Both Bushmen and Pygmies are very small people, though once, long ago, before being driven on to the poorer lands, they may have been as tall as their neighbours. Their skins tend to be lighter in colour than those of the Negroes. The Hottentots also live in the deserts of western South Africa and are neighbours of the Bushmen. Like the Bushmen, they speak languages which contain click-sounds.

At first all the people of Africa lived by hunting and by gathering berries and roots for food. Then, many centuries before the birth of Christ (B.C.), the knowledge of how to cultivate the ground and grow crops and how to tame and breed animals began to spread southwards from Egypt. But the kinds of crops, such as wheat, which grew well in the Nile valley were not suitable for the hotter lands further south. In course of several thousand years people discovered that millet and a kind of rice grew much better than wheat. As the Negroes south of the Sahara, both east and west of the great Lake Chad, began to grow crops of millet and rice, they had better food, and so they increased in numbers and spread over more land.

Millet, rice, and grass grow well in the wide open country we call 'savanna', but they are not suited to the tropical forest lands of Central Africa — the lands of the great Congo River. Then, during the first centuries after the birth of Christ (A.D.), Indonesians began to sail across the Indian Ocean from the tropical islands of the East Indies, and they brought with them yams, bananas, and sweet potatoes, which grow excellently in the hot, wet tropics. As soon as the Negroes began to grow these, they started spreading over the lands north and south of the Equator and increasing in numbers even more. So the Negro people gradually drove the simpler, food-gathering Bushmen, Pygmies, and Hottentots into the poorer lands, and mixed and married with the people from the north who spread southwards. For some 1,500 years or more, until Europeans began to move in, most of Africa south of the Sahara belonged to the Negroes. Today they are gradually winning back the control of the lands which their ancestors used to own.

Africans working on a banana plantation. Yams growing in foreground.

Hottentots. From a print of 1840

4 THE NILE VALLEY

THE NILE, which is the longest river in the world, rises deep in the heart of Africa (see Map p. 21). It begins as a little stream in the highlands of East Africa near the north end of Lake Tanganyika. It flows into Lake Victoria, then into Lake Albert, and then on through the Sudan. In the southern Sudan it wanders through a maze of reeds and swamp which almost block its course, but on the far side it flows more strongly again until it reaches Khartoum, the capital of the Sudan. Near Khartoum it is joined by a big river flowing down from the mountains of Ethiopia. This river is called the Blue Nile, because it is a much darker colour than the main river, which is called the White Nile. The two rivers flow northwards as one great river through the sandy desert into Egypt. Below Cairo, the capital city of Egypt, the Nile separates into several smaller rivers which finally run out into the Mediterranean Sea.

The amount of water in the river varies with the seasons of the year, and depends on the rain which has fallen in the highlands where the White Nile and the Blue Nile rise. In Egypt the river is at its highest each year in the late summer, when the heavy rain that has fallen earlier in the year moves towards the sea in a great muddy tide, flooding the land on both sides. Then gradually the level of the river drops, and the water drains off, leaving behind a layer of rich soil washed down from the mountains.

Thousands of years ago people began to settle in the valley of the Nile and to discover that crops grew very well indeed on the soil left behind when the river floods went down. They also discovered that during the dry season they could water their crops from the river, and they invented simple ways of lifting the water out of the river to irrigate their fields. They grew wheat and barley, vegetables, food-crops for their cattle and sheep and goats and pigs, and flax from which they wove linen. In fact, other peoples, like the

An old Egyptian painting of a man drawing water from the river. The same method is used today

Israelites under Jacob, used to go to Egypt to buy corn when there was famine in their own land. So the Egyptians grew rich.

They knew that their prosperity depended on the river Nile and its flood, for without it the country would be desert. The idea that the river brought renewed life every year was a very important part of their religion. They had a story to explain this. They believed that there were two gods, Osiris and Seth, who were brothers. The brothers had a bitter quarrel about which of them Egypt belonged to, and the wicked Seth killed his brother, cut up the body, and tossed the pieces into the Nile. But in the spring Isis, the wife of Osiris, found the pieces of her husband's body, put them together, and made him come alive again, just as the river brought the crops to life again. Osiris was the god of all growing things, and of the river which brought the water that made them grow.

The King of Egypt was called the Pharaoh, and the people thought of him as being a god. They looked on him as the keeper of the food supply, and thought that the life and health of the country depended on the King's own life and health. They believed that the Pharaoh, while he lived, was the son of Osiris, and that when he died, he came magically to life again in heaven and was united with Osiris himself. They believed that at all costs he must not die altogether, or Egypt itself would die. So they made great preparations for the King's after-life, when his work on earth was finished.

They built magnificent tombs for their Pharaohs, which they felt would be suitable resting-places: these were the pyramids, which are among the most massive buildings men have ever made. When a Pharaoh died, they preserved his body as a mummy, so that it would not decay. They laid it in a burial chamber decorated with pictures of food and drink, of scenes of hunting and feasting, and of other things which the Pharaoh had enjoyed on earth,

An old painting of the god Osiris

so that he could continue them in his after-life. They buried in the tomb the dead Pharaoh's favourite possessions, so that he could go on using them — jewellery, weapons, clothing, and ornaments of all kinds. They then made life-sized statues of all the Pharaohs when they died, so that they could continue to look on this world while living in the next.

It was because of this that the Egyptians became some of the most famous builders and painters and carvers of the ancient world. Because they were rich they could afford to spend much time making these beautiful things, and bringing rich materials, such as gold and ivory, from other countries. Everything depended on the rich mud of the Nile, and the Egyptians came to speak of their country as 'the gift of the river'.

A Pharaoh's golden mummy case

5 THE KINGDOM OF KUSH

The Lion Temple at Naga, one of the cities of Kush

MANY OF THE people who came into ancient Egypt from the Middle East, instead of staying in Egypt, moved further and further up the river Nile, looking for places to settle. Some of them came into the part which is now called the Sudan. Here they mixed with Negro people who were already living there. Most of the light-skinned people from Egypt settled in the northern part, and the people in the southern part were black. The Egyptians called it the land of Kush, or Nubia.

At one time the part of Kush nearest Egypt was ruled by the Egyptian Pharaohs, and towns with Egyptian governors grew up along the Nile. The most important of these towns was Napata, which stood where the river makes a great bend. Opposite Napata, across the river, was a sacred hill on which stood a big temple to the sun. Most people in ancient days thought of the sun as a god, because without the sun nothing would grow. When Egypt grew weaker, and Kush grew strong enough to drive the Egyptian rulers out of their country, the men of Kush made Napata their capital, and they built a great palace for their king.

Life in Napata must have been much like life in any Egyptian town. Everything depended on the yearly flooding of the river, and the same kinds of crops were grown. The ordinary people lived in flat-roofed little houses of mud bricks baked hard in the hot sun. The richer people built their houses round a central courtyard, with one gate in the outer wall. The king's palace and the temples were made of stone. As the people of Kush believed in the same gods as the Egyptians did, they also built fine tombs for their kings, though their pyramids were rather smaller than the Egyptian ones and rather more pointed. Kush grew richer and stronger until, about 600 B.C., she was so strong that she defeated the Egyptians, and for a time the kings of Kush were also the Pharaohs of Egypt. Napata was then one of the great cities of the ancient world.

Then other conquerors, such as the Persians and Alexander the Great from Greece, captured Egypt, and the men of Kush were driven back up the river. They made a new capital further south, at a place called Meroe, which had been an important town for a long time. About the time that Christ was born, Meroe had become a very busy, rich, trading city. Traders travelling to or from the Red Sea or Ethiopia would cross the Nile at Meroe, and trading ships came up and down the Nile. Rain sometimes fell there, so more crops could be grown, and also there were forests. The men of Kush were among the early people to learn the secret of working iron. They smelted the iron with charcoal, made from the forest trees, and even today huge heaps of slag, the waste matter from smelting iron, can be seen near where the city stood. The iron-workers made hoes and spears and axes, which they sold to the merchants in exchange for cotton from India

Remains of the Meröe pyramid tombs. The tops were broken off by robbers hunting for gold

Chapter 6), attacked Meroe and laid it waste. As with many other such cities, the sand of the desert blew over it and buried it, and so it lay for hundreds of years. Then, about 1902, archaeologists began to dig it out again and find out what it had been like. They dug out the stone quay where trading ships on the Nile came in to tie up. They uncovered the remains of palaces and temples and houses, even a swimming-bath rather like those the Romans used to make. They opened up the pyramid tombs and found the treasures that had been buried with the Kings. From the wall paintings and engravings on the pottery bowls and pots, they could tell what the people's houses and possessions were like and could see that the men of Kush were true Africans — very different from the people of Egypt.

A Queen of Kush, from an Egyptian wall painting

and silk from China. As well as this, they made beautiful pottery vases, glass bottles, and silver and copper lamps and bowls, many of which were taken up the Nile and perhaps by caravan across the desert to West Africa. In this way new ideas spread further into Africa.

After many centuries of wealth and prosperity, the Kingdom of Kush, like many other ancient civilizations, came to an end. Armies, especially from the Kingdom of Axum, further east (see

Painted pots and a gold cylinder belonging to King Aspelta of Kush (about 600 B.C.)

17

6 THE KINGDOM OF AXUM

WE READ IN the Old Testament that King Solomon received a visit from the Queen of Sheba, from the southern part of Arabia. There is a very old African story that the King and Queen married and had children, and that the present Emperor of Ethiopia is descended from them. Although this story is not true, it is true that sailors, traders, and explorers from southern Arabia crossed the Red Sea in ancient times and settled in Africa. At first they lived and traded only on the hot coastlands of the Red Sea, but later they began to build towns in the cool highlands of northern Ethiopia, some distance from the coast. The most famous of these towns was Axum.

Axum started as just a small trading-centre, but it gradually increased in importance. Trade-routes from it led into the Nile Valley on the west, and south into Ethiopia; on the east the merchants could trade easily with the sailors of the Indian Ocean through a port on the Red Sea. A Greek sailor in the 1st century A.D. described Axum as the greatest ivory-market in northeastern Africa. The tribes of the bush country inland used to hunt elephants and shoot them with poisoned arrows. Then they would bring the heavy ivory tusks into Axum to sell to the merchants. The merchants would sell the tusks to visiting traders, who would ship them up the Red Sea to Egypt and the countries of the Mediterranean, where ivory was wanted for making jewellery and ornaments.

The merchants also traded in ebony, a hard, black wood which grew in the forests of Ethiopia, and Africans from the inland tribes used to bring gold to Axum, and exchange it for salt and meat. King Solomon may have got the gold for his temple in Jerusalem through the markets of Axum. The merchants of Axum exchanged their goods for many things the traders brought from other countries — sheets of copper, metal swords and spears, wine from Italy, or cotton from India. The markets at Axum must have been very busy and colourful. The traders would bring their laden pack-animals along the well-beaten trade routes up from the coast or the Nile Valley, unload their goods in the markets, and display them. Then they would load the animals again with different goods. Most of the traders were Arabs, but there were also Greeks, and, later, traders from Rome. The Africans from inland would bring their oxen or donkeys laden with ivory, ebony, or gold, and, having done their business, would wander round the magnificent city before returning to their country villages.

As their city became richer, the men of Axum made it more beautiful with splendid stone palaces, temples, and monuments. They borrowed many of their ideas of building from southern Arabia, from which so many of the traders came. In Arabia today we can see tall buildings with walls built up in steps, instead of running straight up and down, and there were buildings like these in Axum. There were also strange, tall pillars of stone called obelisks. A Roman trader, called Julian, described a visit to Axum. The king, he said, lived in a palace with stone towers, and kept tame elephants and giraffes. He wore

The crown of Menelik II from Axum

Slaves carrying ivory to Axum

clothes woven of fine linen and had a rich store of ornaments made with precious stones.

Ideas of farming, as well as building, came from Arabia. The men of Axum learnt to cover the sides of the steep Ethiopian hills with rows of terraces to prevent the good soil from being washed away by the heavy rains. Other peoples further inland copied these ideas, and the remains of these ancient terraces can still be seen in neighbouring parts of Africa.

The merchants of Axum came into competition with the merchants of Meröe in the Nile Valley (see Chapter 5), and from time to time there was war between them. Gradually Axum grew stronger and Meröe weaker, until in the 4th century A.D. a king of Axum called Ousanes finally defeated the armies of Meröe and destroyed their city. On a monument celebrating his victory, the king had written: 'I burnt their towns, and my armies carried off their food and copper and iron and destroyed the statues in their temples.' This king Ousanes was, soon after, converted to Christianity by a priest from Syria, and all his people with him. Early in his reign his bronze and gold coins had pictures of the moon and stars; later, they had the Christian Cross. People even now dig up these coins occasionally in the fields around Axum. Ethiopia has been a Christian country ever since.

In the 7th century, Axum, like Meröe, began to decay and the busy prosperous city became deserted, buried, and overgrown, showing little trace of its past glories. Now, also like Meröe, archaeologists have uncovered a great deal of it and, one way and another, have been able to build up a picture of what it was once like.

A coin of King Ousanes

7 SOME AFRICAN BIRDS

AFRICA HAS A wonderful number of interesting birds — in the lakes and marshes, on the open grassland, or in the tropical forests. Everyone knows about the Ostriches, which may be 7 or 8 feet tall, live in the open grassland, and run as fast as galloping horses, but cannot fly. These are some of the other interesting birds.

THE AFRICAN LILY-TROTTER

This is a bird of the inland lakes and ponds of Africa. It lives in places where stretches of still water are covered with water-lilies and other water plants. It has extraordinarily long toes, which distribute its weight so well that it can walk on the floating leaves without sinking, while it hunts for the insects and snails which are its food. A Lily-trotter's nest is a mound of water-weed, and there it lays three or four shiny brown eggs with black, wavy markings on them.

THE SNAKE-BIRD OR AFRICAN DARTER

This bird also lives on the inland lakes. It is a large bird, nearly 3 feet tall. It has been given its name, Snake-bird, because of its appearance when swimming: it looks very much like a snake in motion, as it moves through the water with its body submerged, and only its head and neck, swaying from side to side, showing above the surface. The Snake-bird builds its nest of sticks in the branches of trees, in colonies with other water birds.

A Honey-guide by an African bee-hive

THE GREATER HONEY-GUIDE

The Honey-guide is a bird of the forest. Like a Cuckoo, it lays its eggs in other birds' nests. When the eggs hatch, the young Honey-guides use the sharp hooks on their bills to kill any other baby birds which may be in the nest. The name Honey-guide comes from a remarkable service which these birds and the people who live in the forest give each other: the birds actually lead men to trees where wild bees have stored their honey. The men smoke out the bees and collect the honey, and then the birds eat the grubs and the honey-comb.

Lily-trotters   Snake-bird

The Black-necked Weaver

The weavers are a large group of small birds, about the size of finches, which live in the bush country of Africa. They get their name from the way they make their nests: usually one bird flies out and collects pieces of grass and plants and brings them back to the other bird, which weaves them into the nest. Weaver-birds usually live in colonies, their nests clustered in the branches of a group of trees. The Black-necked Weaver, however, is a less social bird than most of the others. It builds a very unusual nest, made of tightly-woven pieces of grass and twigs, like the other Weaver-birds' nests, but with a long tunnel entrance, which hangs down below. This kind of entrance probably keeps snakes from getting into the nest and killing the young birds.

Black-necked Weavers on their nest

The Secretary Bird

This tall, elegant bird stalks across the plains looking for snakes, lizards, mice, and grasshoppers, which are its food. It is called the Secretary Bird because its crest feathers, which stick out behind its head, look very much like an old-fashioned quill pen stuck behind a secretary's ear. Its nest is usually a great mattress of sticks, woven round the top branches of a thorn-tree, and the female lays two white eggs there in each breeding season.

A Marabou Stork

The Marabou Stork

This is a huge, ugly bird, over 5 feet tall, which is often to be seen on the plains in Africa. Whenever lions have killed and eaten some animal, and the vultures have gathered to devour the remains, the Marabou Stork is likely to come down from his untidy nest and join them. He is, in fact, a useful scavenger of the grasslands.

A Secretary Bird

8 THE SAHARA DESERT

A Bedouin camp in the Sahara

RIGHT ACROSS north Africa stretches the largest desert in the world — the Sahara. It is 3,000 miles from west to east and 1,000 miles from north to south. Parts of it are covered with soft sand which the wind blows into strange shapes. In other parts there is hard, red sandstone, with high, rocky places and even ranges of mountains. These are cut by valleys, called wadis, along which, ages ago, rivers used to run, but which are now dry. In some parts, particularly in the south, where it rains a little in the spring, grass grows for a few months; and here shepherds graze their camels, goats, and sheep.

In the Sahara the sun burns fiercely during the day, and is so hot that anything made of metal becomes much too hot to touch. But when the sun sets, it very quickly becomes cold, sometimes even freezing; the air is clear, and the stars shine

An oasis in the Sahara

very brightly. Usually a warm, dry wind is blowing, and sometimes there are terrible sandstorms, when the wind whips up great clouds of sand which darken the sky. Everyone has to take shelter; camels kneel down with their backs to the storm, and their riders throw cloaks over their heads and crouch down in the shelter of their beasts. The storm may last an hour or less or it may go on for several days.

In parts of the desert there may be no rain at all for several years, and then perhaps a sudden heavy shower. In other parts there will be showers occasionally, especially in the spring. As soon as there is rain, grass and wild flowers spring up very quickly, but before long the hot sun dries them up again. In fact, in many parts of the desert there is plenty of water, but usually deep underground. In some places this underground water comes near the surface, and wells can be dug or the water comes up in natural springs. These places are called oases, and date-palms, vegetables, and grain can be grown, and towns are built. The tracks across the desert go from one oasis to another, but there are often 100 miles or more of dry desert between them.

From the beginning of history, in spite of the difficulties, people have travelled across the desert, navigating by the stars. In places drawings were cut in the rock by ancient peoples showing carts pulled by horses or donkeys. The places where these drawings have been found show that there used to be two main routes across the desert, both starting from the river Niger near Timbuktu (see Chapter 10); one led north-east, reaching the Mediterranean near Tripoli, and the other ran west and then north, over the Atlas Mountains towards Gibraltar. These ancient routes were used mostly by traders, but also by conquering armies.

Today the people who live on the grasslands of the southern Sahara are mostly Negroes; but the real desert people are the Berbers, who live and farm in mountain villages to the north, the camel-riding Touareg of the central Sahara (see Chapter 10), and the Bedouin Arabs. 'Bedouin' means 'wanderer', and these people have no settled homes, but move from one grazing ground to another, living in black tents made of woven goats' hair. They carry all their belongings on camel-back, and breed camels, sheep, and goats. The men wear white shirts, brown camel-hair cloaks, and bright head-cloths held in place by a piece of rope. The women wear long, dark, cotton dresses and black head-cloths, and often have their faces veiled, for they are Moslems. Each tribe is led by its Sheikh, and each has special

A night view of burning gas at oil-wells in Algeria

grazing areas so that they do not interfere with each other.

Nowadays there are some good roads across the desert, and even the tracks are well marked and firm enough for motor traffic. So camels are not as important as they used to be. Also, now that oil wells are being dug in the Sahara, many of the Bedouin are giving up their wandering lives and settling down to work in the oil towns.

9 THE KINGDOM OF GHANA

ANYONE TRAVELLING south from the Sahara Desert soon begins to find the country less barren: there is more grass and trees begin to appear — at first small and stunted bushes, but then taller and more shady trees. This grassland country, lying between the desert and the hot, wet, tropical forest further south, was called by the Arabs the Sudan, or country of black men.

During what European history books sometimes called the Dark Ages, from about the 5th to the 11th centuries, Africans were building up trading centres in the Sudan. As more and more traders came from the Nile Valley or across the Sahara Desert, these trading towns grew bigger and richer. Then, as one town managed to defeat its neighbour in battle, some of them developed into powerful kingdoms. The first of these kingdoms was Ghana, which lay at the western end of the Sudan. Its people had learnt how to smelt iron and make iron tools and weapons; and with their iron spears and swords, the soldiers of Ghana easily defeated their neighbours, who had only wooden weapons.

The most important trade in the markets of Ghana was in gold and salt. The Negroes who lived near the upper part of the rivers Niger and Senegal were gold miners. The laws of Ghana laid down that all big lumps of gold found in the country belonged to the king, but that the people themselves might keep the little bits or gold dust. The king of Ghana sold the gold to the merchants from the Sahara, who themselves brought salt to Ghana. People in hot countries, who sweat a good deal, need to eat plenty of salt to keep healthy. There was no salt in the Kingdom of Ghana, and so the merchants found a ready market for their salt. The king of Ghana made the merchants pay a tax on every donkey-load of salt which came into the kingdom. The markets of Ghana sold other goods too. The merchants brought cloth and metal goods from North Africa and exchanged them for ivory and skins and slaves (see Chapter 14). In all these ways the kings of Ghana grew very rich.

Though they were pagans, the kings ruled their country well, and they learnt much from the Moslem Arab merchants. In 1067, the year after the Battle of Hastings, an Arab writer wrote an account of what the court of Ghana was like. The king, he wrote, used to hold public meetings, at which any of his people might bring complaints or ask for judgements to settle quarrels. A council meeting was announced by the beating of a big drum made from a hollowed log. The king sat in a pavilion attended by ten pages carrying shields and gilded swords. On his right sat the princes of the kingdom in splendid robes with

The Court of the King of Ghana in 1067

gold thread woven in their hair. On the ground in front of him sat the city governor and the king's advisors. Guarding the gate were the king's fierce guard dogs, with their gold and silver collars, who were trained never to leave the gate unguarded. When the people approached the king, they fell on their knees and threw dust on their heads to show humble respect. Then those who asked for justice stood and humbly presented their case, and the king, with the help of his advisors, passed judgement.

The people of Ghana, like other West Africans, built their houses of wood and clay and thatch. But the merchants from North Africa, who were allowed to build their own city about 6 miles from the king's capital, built in stone, as they were accustomed to do in their own countries. Stone lasts better than wood and clay, and so, though there is now no trace left of the king's city, archaeologists believe that the ruins of a stone town they have discovered about 200 miles north of Bamako on the Niger, must be the merchants' city.

Ghana, like other great kingdoms, was finally defeated by more powerful neighbours and came to an end. The country was ruled for a long time by African and then European conquerors. But when, in 1957, the people of the Gold Coast became independent, they called their new nation Ghana in memory of the ancient kingdom.

10 TIMBUKTU

Timbuktu, from a picture by Barth in 1853.
In the background is the Moslem Mosque

PEOPLE IN ENGLAND, if they wanted to say that a place was a very long way away, used to say that it was 'as far as Timbuktu'. This was because the town lay in the Sahara Desert, and until the 20th century, very few Europeans had been there or knew anything about it, except from stories. Once, it was a great city; now it is a dusty, hot, sleepy little town near the river Niger in the Republic of Mali (see map, p. 11).

Timbuktu first became an important town in the 11th century, about the time of William the Conqueror. It became important because it was a meeting place of caravan routes across the desert from north African cities such as Cairo, Tunis, or Fez. The great camel caravans would meet at Timbuktu and rest there. They might sell their goods in the Timbuktu markets and load their camels with fresh goods to take back across the desert to their own towns; or they might put their merchandize on to boats to go down the river Niger.

The principal traders in the 11th and 12th centuries were Arabs, who were Moslems — followers of the prophet Mohammed. They brought their religion with them, and so most of the Negro people of this part of Africa became Moslems. They are still Moslems today. All Moslems wish, if they can, to make a pilgrimage to Mecca in Arabia, and so wealthy Negro rulers, such as the Emperor Mansa Musa of Mali, would travel by the caravan routes across Africa to the Arab countries. Mansa Musa went on a pilgrimage to Mecca in 1324, taking a great deal of gold with him, for Mali was rich in gold. He stayed for a time in Cairo in Egypt, and persuaded many Arab scholars to come back to Timbuktu with him. These scholars settled there, and gradually others came to join them, and so the Moslem University of Timbuktu became a very important centre of learning. All Arabs knew of the University of Timbuktu; but still no Europeans went there.

Among Mansa Musa's scholars was an architect who taught the Negroes how to build in brick, and he built several fine palaces and mosques. Before then, the houses and mosques had been built of sun-baked clay. The streets of the town were narrow to give them shade from the burning sun, and the houses had flat roofs, like most houses in hot, dry countries.

Timbuktu was at its greatest in the 15th and 16th centuries, when it was the business centre of a large Negro Empire under a strong ruler called Askia the Great. About 1520, a young Arab from Fez in Morocco came with his uncle to visit Askia the Great. The young man wrote an account of Timbuktu as he saw it. 'The inhabitants are very rich,' he wrote, 'especially the foreigners who have settled there... There are many judges, doctors, and holy men... There is a big demand for hand-written books from North Africa, and the book trade in Timbuktu brings greater profits than any other kind of business.' There were also historians in the University, whose books still exist and from which we learn about the early history of western Africa.

After about 1600, Timbuktu became less important, partly because it was attacked by enemies, and partly because the caravan trade across the Sahara grew less as merchants from Europe explored the west coast of Africa and traded by ship from the coasts.

Touareg in the desert

Touareg traders entering Timbuktu

In 1800 fierce wild tribes from the desert, called Touaregs, captured Timbuktu. The Touaregs were always carrying out raids on caravan parties, villages, or towns. They rode camels and fought with splendid swords and spears. They captured camels from those they attacked, for every Touareg wanted to own as many camels as he could. The Touaregs were tall, fine-looking men, and they wore cotton robes with black hoods over their heads, which covered their faces except for slits for their eyes. No Touareg was ever seen without his veil.

For nearly 100 years Timbuktu was deserted. Then the French conquered much of north-west Africa, and Timbuktu again became a trading centre. Now the trade comes by lorry along desert roads, instead of by camel. There is an airport, and from July to January, when the river is full of water, boats on the Niger bring visitors to the town from Bamako, the capital of Mali. But Timbuktu is no longer a great centre of learning, as it was in earlier days.

11 ALONG THE RIVER NIGER

PEOPLE IN EUROPE had known for a long time that there was a great river running through Negro lands in West Africa; but it was a mystery river, and no-one knew where it started or whether it ever reached the sea. Arab traders, who had seen the river when they went to Timbuktu, saw that it was flowing inland, apparently away from the sea, and people suggested that it might flow right across Africa into the Nile. Other people thought that it might end in some huge inland lake, or even flow into an underground channel in the Sahara Desert and come out into the Mediterranean Sea. In 1797 a young Scottish doctor called Mungo Park set out from the west coast of Africa to see if he could solve the mystery. The story of his adventures is told in Book 2 in this series.

Mungo Park discovered that the Niger rises about 150 miles from the Atlantic coast in the

A Benin bronze figure of a Portuguese soldier

eastern slopes of the mountains of Guinea, and flows north-eastwards. He travelled along it to the ancient market town of Bamako, the capital of Mali. After Bamako, the river is almost lost in a series of small lakes and marshes, which once had been a great inland lake. Now the marshes have been drained and a big dam built

The present Oba of Benin, who was enthroned in 1964

so that there is plenty of water to irrigate the farms. The farmers now grow fine crops of rice on small plots of land — enough to feed the people of Mali and to export thousands of tons every year to other countries.

Mungo Park, after he had passed Timbuktu, discovered that the Niger makes a huge bend and flows southwards through dry, hot, sandy country. The few people that live there live near the river, growing groundnuts and keeping herds of cattle, sheep, and goats.

After travelling some 1700 miles down the river, Mungo Park and his three companions reached some very dangerous rapids, called the Bussa Rapids, and there their boat was wrecked and they were all drowned. So Park never found out where the Niger finally goes to. But some 30 years later another explorer, called Richard Lander, took up the journey from where Park had been killed, and traced the Niger through dense tropical forests, until it breaks up into several streams and flows into the Gulf of Guinea (see map p. 11). Altogether, the Niger is 2,600 miles long, longer than any other African river except the Nile and the Congo. During all this great length there are hardly any bridges across it. Everyone crosses by ferry.

When the Portuguese first came to West Africa in the 15th century (see Chapter 13), the forest lands all along the west coast as far as the mouth of the Congo belonged to several different Negro kingdoms. The most famous of these is the Kingdom of Benin. Its capital lies about 80 miles west of the Niger, and at its greatest, the kingdom stretched east and west of the river.

When the Portuguese first visited it some 500 years ago, the city of Benin was a large town, several miles round, and defended by a deep moat. Its people were famous because of their skilful and beautiful metal work and ivory carving. Among the things they made were splendid bronze portraits of their kings (who were called Obas), ivory masks with human or leopard faces, and statues of kings and their courtiers, horsemen, horn-players, or animals, especially leopards. A leopard was a symbol for a king.

The Portuguese made friends with the Oba of Benin, and the two countries traded with each other. But the trade was mostly in slaves (see Chapter 14). Benin remained an independent kingdom until the end of the 19th century; but in its later years the people followed a very cruel and bloodthirsty religion. The powerful rulers in the country were the priests, and they shut their country off from the rest of the world, and they taught their people that their High Spirit or god needed human sacrifices. In 1897 the British sent an army to conquer Benin because some English officers had been murdered. The British were so horrified at the terrible things they found that they called Benin the 'city of blood', and they took control of the kingdom and put a stop to the human sacrifices.

Today Benin is part of Nigeria, and the city has modern churches, schools, and clinics, and an Institute for studying farming, in particular the growing of oil palms. Visitors go to Benin today to look at the Oba's palace and the street of the bronze-workers.

A ferry on the River Niger. The man on the left is cooking and selling *kebabs* — pieces of meat on sticks

12 THE TUG-OF-WAR

Mouse-birds

AFRICA HAS A vast number of folk stories, and many are about animals. This is a very popular one, which may have first come from West Africa, and is now told in many parts of Africa south of the Sahara. The mouse-bird is a common African bird to be seen almost everywhere, as a sparrow is to be seen in Europe.

A mouse-bird and his wife lived in a tall tree near the forest edge. They had three babies in the nest, quite well-grown and nearly ready to fly. For many days they had worked hard collecting food for the family. Then, late one afternoon, they flew down to the river to bathe.

They chose a shallow pool under some trees and hopped into the water, splashing happily. Suddenly an angry shout came from the undergrowth at the foot of the trees. 'Stop that!' it said. 'Who told you that you could bathe in my pool?' A huge crocodile came slowly into view and stared angrily at the mouse-birds.

The mouse-birds were extremely frightened but the cock bird answered quite bravely, 'It isn't your pool. Anyone can bathe in this river. I've often bathed here before, and I'm going to keep on coming.' 'Oh no you're not,' replied the crocodile. 'This pool belongs to me and my family. If you come here again I shall kill you. I'm much stronger than you are. One flick of my tail and you'd be just a pile of feathers.'

'I don't think you're any stronger than I am,' said the mouse-bird. But if you like we'll have a trial of strength. Come to my tree in the morning when the sun is above the forest. If you win, I promise you I'll never bathe in this pool again.' 'All right,' said the crocodile, 'I'll be there.'

As the mouse-bird and his wife flew back to their nest, they tried to think of some way to defeat the crocodile; but no ideas came. They fed the babies and settled sadly down for the night. Suddenly there was a heavy bump which shook the tree so hard that one of the babies almost fell out. The mouse-bird peered down through the branches. 'Be careful, whoever you are,' he called out. 'You nearly shook us out of the tree altogether.' 'You've no business to be in that tree at all,' said a deep voice. A grey trunk

reached up and pulled aside one of the branches. A big bull elephant was standing under the tree. 'This path is mine,' the elephant went on, 'and I don't like strangers living on it. I'm afraid I must ask you to move.'

The mouse-bird, although he was very frightened, answered with his usual cocky courage, 'I don't want to move. Anyone can live in these trees. We've made our nest here, and we're going to stay.' 'Oh no you're not,' said the elephant. 'This path belongs to me and my family. If you stay here I shall kill you. I'm much stronger than you are. Why, with one of my feet, I could flatten you to nothing.'

'I don't think you're any stronger than I am,' said the mouse-bird. 'But if you like we'll have a trial of strength. Come here to my tree in the morning when the sun is above the forest. If you win I promise you I'll leave this tree for ever.' 'I'll be here,' said the elephant.

When the elephant had gone, the mouse-bird said to his wife, 'I think we can teach these animals a lesson. You fly that way and bring all the help you can, and I'll do the same this way.' Before long, hundreds of mouse-birds flew to the forest path, and all through the night they worked, plaiting a long, sturdy rope out of many strands of the climbing plants of the forest. Soon after dawn they finished and flew away, leaving the family in the nest to await the arrival of the crocodile and the elephant.

When the sun rose above the forest, the mouse-bird heard a trumpeting down the path, and flew to meet the elephant. 'Do you see this rope?' he asked. 'We'll have a tug-of-war to see which of us is the stronger. Take this end, face that way down the path, and when I say, "Pull!", pull as hard as you can.' 'Very well,' said the elephant, and turning round, pulled the rope over his shoulder. The mouse-bird flew back down the path towards the river to meet the crocodile. 'Do you see this rope?' he asked. 'Take this end, face the river, and when I say, "Pull!", pull as hard as you can. We'll soon find out which of us is the stronger.' 'Very well,' said the crocodile, and gripped the rope with his strong teeth.

Then the mouse-bird perched on the middle of the rope, where neither the elephant nor the crocodile could see him. 'Are you ready?' he shouted. 'One, two, three, pull!' The rope creaked as the two great beasts pulled with all their might, but although they went on pulling for an hour, it did not move an inch in either direction. 'You'll have to do better than that,' called the mouse-bird, sounding fresh and cheerful. 'It feels to me as if you're tiring. Would you like a short rest?' 'Yes,' gasped the crocodile and the elephant together, both letting go.

The mouse-bird flew down the path towards the crocodile, who was lying panting on the ground. 'It's all right,' groaned the crocodile, 'you can go on bathing in that pool.' 'Thank you,' said the mouse-bird. Then he flew to the other end of the rope, where the exhausted elephant was leaning against a tree. 'You can go on living here,' he said. 'Thank you,' said the mouse-bird. 'My wife and I will be very pleased to see you whenever you pass this way.'

13 THE PORTUGUESE IN WEST AFRICA

A Portuguese chart of the West African coast, 1502

Diego Cam's pillar

ABOUT 500 YEARS AGO, the people of Europe wanted to find a sea-route to India and the East Indies because they wanted to trade there. The old routes across land from the Mediterranean Sea were no longer open to them because the Turks had conquered this land and would not allow Christians to go through.

The first sailors to search for a way of reaching the East by sea were the Portuguese. Prince Henry of Portugal felt sure that a way to the East could be found by sailing round Africa, and the story of his expeditions is told in Book 2 of this Series. But no Europeans knew anything about Africa: they had no idea how far they would have to sail before they found a way round, nor what terrible things might happen to them if they sailed too far. However, gradually, year by year, the Portuguese sailors worked their way further and further south, and as they discovered that the sea did not boil as they sailed southwards, nor were white men turned into black men, nor did they meet any fearsome sea monsters, they grew bolder and more enterprising. By 1460, the year Prince Henry died, they had reached as far south as the country which is now Sierre Leone (see Map p. 11).

When the sailors found that the coast of Africa was turning eastwards, they must have begun to get very hopeful. Perhaps it would not be so far now before they could get right round Africa and reach the Indian Ocean and the East. But how mistaken they were! After they had sailed past the mouth of the great river Niger, they found that the coastline turned south again. And by 1482 a Portuguese captain called Diego Cam reached as far south as the Equator. But still there was no sign that the coast of Africa would ever come to an end.

As they were seeking a sea route round Africa the captains of the Portuguese ships took every possible chance of trading with the people along the coast, and also of converting them to Christianity, as Prince Henry had ordered them. When they reached what is now the coast of Ghana, they landed and built a fort to act as a trading post. A few years later, another ship stopped at the mouth of the Niger, and the sailors met some of the Negroes of the Kingdom of Benin (see Chapter 11). They were surprised to find that these Africans belonged to organized kingdoms, and that the country was not inhabited only by savages and wild animals. The Portuguese visited the city of Benin and even built a church there. They found that the Africans grew pepper, which was one of the spices which Europeans wanted from the East. So they traded with the people of Benin and others of the West African kingdoms.

After he had sailed across the Equator, Diego Cam arrived at the mouth of the river Congo. He set up a carved pillar there to show how far he had sailed, and he called the river the 'River of the Pillar'. He sailed some way up the river and landed on the southern bank. There he found another African kingdom, and the king, called Manicongo or 'King of the Congo People', was very friendly. The capital of the Congo kingdom was about 150 miles inland in grassland country in what is now Angola. The people lived in rectangular grass huts and farmed cattle, sheep, pigs, and chickens. They knew how to work iron and copper, and the iron-smiths, who were very honoured people in the country, made axes for cutting down trees and hoes for cultivating the fields of millet. The Portuguese gave the people maize seed, which the sailors had recently brought from America, and soon they were growing maize as well.

The king of the Congo was delighted with what the Portuguese brought them, and he soon became a Christian. He begged the Portuguese to send them priests and farmers and masons to teach his people. Soon churches and schools were being built in stone — so many churches that the capital city came to be called 'the city of church bells'. Also the king sent his sons and other young men to Portugal to learn European ways. The kingdom of the Congo was prosperous and peaceful.

But as the Portuguese sailed further south (in Book 2 we read how Vasco da Gama finally sailed right round Africa and reached India), they

Portuguese trading with Africans

lost interest in the little kingdom of the Congo. Other countries also sent ships to Africa, and trading posts were set up in many places along the West African coast. The Europeans began trading in slaves (see Chapter 14) as well as in gold and ivory. The little Congo kingdom was attacked by other tribes, and like many African kingdoms, it fell into decay.

A Portuguese church in Angola

14 THE SLAVE TRADE IN WEST AFRICA

IF YOU WERE TO travel today in the West Indies or in the southern states of the U.S.A., you would notice that a great many of the people are Negroes, looking very much like Negroes from Ghana or Nigeria in Africa. You might wonder how Negroes came to be living so very far from Africa, right on the other side of the Atlantic Ocean. These Negroes have, in fact, been living in the Americas for many generations, ever since their ancestors were first brought from Africa as slaves.

From the beginning of history there have been people in many parts of the world who owned slaves, and most of them saw nothing wrong in one person owning another person. There had been slavery all over Africa for centuries (see Chapter 32). A tribe which defeated another tribe in war used to make slaves of the prisoners it captured; or people who committed crimes sometimes lost their freedom: a man who got badly into debt, for example, might become the slave of the man to whom he owed money or goods.

The Portuguese, who were the first Europeans to explore down the coast of West Africa, discovered that they could buy slaves from the African chiefs. In the 16th and 17th centuries, when Europeans began to settle in the New World, labourers were needed to work on the huge farms, or plantations, growing sugar cane or tobacco. So the Portuguese took the slaves across the Atlantic and sold them to the settlers. Soon other nations began to trade in slaves as well, and before long England had a large slave trade. The merchants of Bristol and Liverpool worked out a system which was very profitable: they used to load their ships in England with cloth, guns, and gin, and carry these to West Africa, where they exchanged them for slaves. They carried the slaves across the Atlantic and sold them to the farmers in exchange for sugar and tobacco. Then they carried the sugar and tobacco back to England to sell there. This trade in slaves between West Africa and America went on for more than 300 years, and altogether nearly 15 million Africans were taken from their homes to work on plantations across the sea. The European merchants, the African chiefs, and the American farmers all grew rich at the expense of the wretched slaves. But every year Africa lost thousands of her best young men and women, and the chiefs waged war with each other with the guns the traders brought.

Many of the slaves were taken from the coast of what is now Nigeria in West Africa. The slave trader would make a headquarters on an old ship, which was run aground in an inlet at the mouth of the River Niger. When a ship arrived from Europe, the trader and the captain of the ship would visit a local chief to bargain over a cargo of slaves. The bargaining might last for

A slave trader and local chief bargaining for slaves

Slaves going on board a slave ship

several days, with much fierce arguing, but the chiefs were eager to get the goods the captain had brought with him, and soon 200–300 slaves would be bought for guns, iron bars, gin, beads, and cloth. The price for a man slave might be twelve bars of iron, and nine bars for a woman.

The slaves were then marched to the coast and crowded into barracks to wait until the ship's carpenter had fitted slave-decks in the hold where the cargo had been stored. Then, chained together, they were loaded aboard and packed on to the slave-decks so tightly that often there was hardly room to lie down. During the 5-week trip across the Atlantic, they usually had to stay below decks most of the time, with little to eat or drink and no way to wash or exercise. In these terrible conditions, many of them died before they ever reached America. If ever the slaves were allowed to come on deck for fresh air, the captains were so afraid that they would mutiny that they kept cannons pointed at them all the time ready to shoot at the least sign of trouble. But some captains began to realize that they would get a better price for their slaves in America if they arrived in good condition, and that it was a waste of money to let a slave die, as it would be to let a horse or cow die. So on many ships the slaves' conditions were not much worse than those of the ordinary seamen.

As time went on, people in Europe, especially in England, began to realize how wicked this trade was, and people such as William Wilberforce and the Prime Minister, William Pitt, demanded that the slave trade be stopped. At last, in 1807, the British Parliament passed a law forbidding Englishmen to buy or sell slaves, and soon Holland and America passed similar laws. Ships which used to load slaves from the Nigerian coast began to take on palm-oil instead, which English factories used for making soap. But it took a long time to bring the slave trade to an end. While there was still demand for labourers on the plantations, traders used to smuggle slaves across the Atlantic. When slavery in America ceased altogether about 100 years ago, no more slaves were taken from West Africa.

15 MARY KINGSLEY TRAVELS IN WEST AFRICA

Mary Kingsley exploring Gabon forest

WHEN MARY KINGSLEY decided to travel to West Africa in 1893, everyone she talked to — doctors, scientists, and friends — tried to persuade her not to go. In those days West Africa was often called the 'deadliest place on earth', for it was still thought to be full of wild animals, fierce savages, and terrible diseases — an impossible country for women to go to. Also, Mary Kingsley was not an experienced traveller: she had been outside England only once, for a very short time, and the little she knew about West Africa she had read in books. But Mary, who wanted to study the people and the natural life of Africa, was determined to make the trip. So, all alone, in 1893, she sailed for Africa, and during the next few years, she travelled through several West African countries, sometimes with traders or missionaries, sometimes only with native guides, and sometimes just by herself. Dressed in a high-necked blouse and long, black skirt, and carrying her umbrella, she strode through the African forests, when most English women were staying meekly at home.

Mary Kingsley wrote a wonderful book about her adventures in Africa, called *Travels in West Africa*. In this book she describes the people she met and their many strange customs, the forests, rivers, and mountains which she explored, and the many kinds of fish, insects, and other living things which she collected and brought back to the Natural History Museum in London. One of her favourite regions was the French Congo, now the country of Gabon, just above the mouth of the Congo River. There were many cannibal tribes in the Congo, and the fiercest of them all was the Fan (or Fang) tribe. Mary Kingsley tells about her first visit to a Fan village. One day, when she had been exploring alone in the forest, looking for butterflies and beetles, and even deadly snakes, for her collections, she lost her way in some thick bush. Suddenly she slipped, tumbled down a muddy hillside, and fell right through the roof of a Fan hut, landing by the fireside. The Fan family was surprised and frightened, and Mary could not explain very well what had happened, because she knew only one word in the Fan language. But when she gave them three handkerchiefs, some tobacco, and a knife, they decided she was friendly and let her go. An old sea captain, who had been in Africa for many years, had once told her, 'Be afraid of an African if you can't help it, but never show it anyhow.' Mary was often frightened of the wild and naked men she met in her wanderings, but she always believed that with kindness and sympathy many problems between white men and black men could be solved.

She learned a great deal more about the Fans and how to get along with them when she made a very dangerous journey through a part of the Fan country which had never been explored before. She found that, in those parts which no white missionaries or officials had visited, the primitive people were more friendly and more willing to teach her their customs.

Mary won the respect of many peoples on the coast on one occasion when she climbed the greatest mountain of the Cameroons, Mungo Mah Lobeh, or 'the throne of thunder'. Only two other Englishmen had reached the top of this mountain; many had failed, mostly because their African guides were frightened of the terrible storms and cold on the mountain, and would run away. Mary had to climb the peak by herself, while her guides waited in camp about half-way up the mountain, but at least they did not desert her. She always thought of them first, wrapping them in blankets, giving them rum and tea, and watching over them at night so that they did not roll into their fires while they slept. In *Travels in West Africa* she wrote about this adventure, 'I think if I had collapsed, they would have lain down and died in the cold, sleety rain.'

Another of her most exciting expeditions was a trip up the Ogowe river, when she and eight Africans canoed through dangerous rapids, far from the nearest white settlement. Few white men or even Africans had ever made this trip, but Mary was anxious to collect certain kinds of fish which lived in this river above the rapids. She tells how, on their first night in the rapids, they could not find the Fan village where they had planned to stop. So she and her crew paddled on in the dark, sometimes tipping over or getting stuck on great, jagged rocks, sometimes being caught in whirlpools so that the canoe was turned around and swept down the stream backwards.

Mary Kingsley letting the leopard out of the trap

The wild animals prowling in the forests or near the rivers made these journeys into the heart of the Congo even more dangerous; but Mary tried to show them, too, that she was not frightened. One day she let a leopard out of a trap, because it was hurting itself against the cage bars; and when the freed animal turned to attack her, she looked it in the eye, stamped her foot, and snapped, 'Go home, you fool!', and the startled leopard ran off into the bush. Another time an 8-foot-long crocodile tried to climb into the canoe where she was sitting. Mary scrambled to the other end of the canoe to keep it from tipping over, and kept banging the crocodile on the snout with her paddle, until it gave up and waddled away.

In 1900 Mary Kingsley volunteered to help nurse soldiers wounded in the South African Boer War (see Chapter 22). A few months later, tired and weak from nursing night and day, she died of a fever when she was only 38. Mary Kingsley is remembered for the high-hearted and adventurous way in which she tried to learn about Africa, to teach her countrymen about the life and people of their West African colonies, and to win justice and understanding for white man and black man alike.

16 SENEGAL

THIS IS THE MOST westerly of all the countries of Africa (see map, p. 11). Until 1960 it was part of the French West-African empire, and its big city, Dakar, was the capital of this large empire. A number of French people still live in Dakar, and the people of Senegal all speak French, do their business in French, and learn their lessons in school in French, although they have their own native languages as well.

Most of the people of Senegal are Negroes. When the country became an independent republic, the first President was a Negro called Léopold Senghor, and he has been one of the best leaders of the new African states. He went to school in Dakar, and then he went to Paris University, where he won high honours. He worked as a teacher in France and also fought as a soldier, and for a time was a member of the French Parliament. Then he came back to his own country and was chosen to lead her when she became independent. As well as being a scholar and a ruler, he is a writer and poet. When he came back to Senegal, he wrote: 'I come, hoping to forget about Europe in the quiet heart of my home.'

The Negroes of Senegal are tall and slender, and have the darkest skins of all African Negroes. They used to be divided into many different tribes, with their own rulers, languages, and customs; and still today, though they are all under the same government and speak French, they keep their tribal chiefs. The largest tribe is the Wolof tribe. They are great talkers and story-tellers (see Chapter 12). The Chiefs still keep groups of musicians among their attendants, who play drums and African violins and guitars, and are rather like the jesters of English courts in the Middle Ages. Wolof women look splendid in their best clothes — long brilliantly-coloured dresses with round necks and wide sleeves, and slips of coloured cloth over the top. They often build their hair up over wigs made of tree bark, and tie bright head-scarves over it. They wear a great deal of jewellery — rings, pendants, ear-rings, and bracelets — made of gold if their husbands can afford it.

People who live in Dakar live in modern houses, but in the country the houses are usually made of mud with thatched roofs. Most of the people are farmers, and the chief crop is groundnuts (which we often call monkey-nuts or pea-nuts, and are not really nuts at all). The best groundnut-farmers are the Serer tribe, who live inland from Dakar where the soil is fertile. Groundnuts grow on small annual plants, not unlike kidney beans, with hairy, egg-shaped leaves and yellow flowers which form seed-pods. When the pods are formed, the plants bend over

Women of the Wolof tribe

Groundnut plant

naturally, so that the pods are pushed into the ground. There, they ripen, until they are dug out at harvest time. Inside each crinkly pod are two or more round, brownish-red seeds, and these are the 'nuts'. Thousands of tons of these are sent from the little farms to the factories in Dakar, where they are crushed. A valuable oil comes from them, which the Africans use as cooking oil, and which is used to make margarine or soap. Peanut butter is made from them, and they are very nourishing food eaten roasted or in soups and curries. After the oil has been extracted, the rest is made into cattle-cake which is excellent animal food.

Senegal makes most of its money out of groundnuts. But the farmers also grow millet in the north and rice in the south to feed their families, and on the coast there are many fishermen, for the seas are rich in fish. The factories in Dakar are now making phosphate fertilizers.

Senegal is very hot, but for much of the year it is a dry heat and so quite agreeable. But in the

A Senegal village. The tree is a baobab

summer months, when most of the rain falls, Senegal is unpleasantly hot for Europeans. Most of the country is flat and sandy, and in the north it is almost desert for it is not far from the Sahara Desert. There is little grass and only the kinds of trees which will grow in dry places. There are strange trees called baobabs, which have short, thick trunks, twisting branches, and hardly any leaves. The trunks are sometimes 25 or 30 feet across, and they hold water in pockets in their trunks. The Africans sometimes hollow them out and make houses out of the living trees. They have even used them as prisons. Further south, where there is much more rain, there are tropical forests.

Dakar is far the biggest city — an important city for so small a country. It is the chief port on the whole west coast of Africa and has a very important airport. It has fine modern buildings gleaming white in the strong sun, and handsome tree-lined streets.

A market in Dakar

17 DR. AGGREY THE SCHOOLMASTER

WHEN JAMES AGGREY was only 23 years old, in 1898, he was already headmaster of the Cape Coast school in Ghana. He made the 400 pupils in his school work hard, but every now and then he used to tell them stories. This is one he liked to tell:

Once a farmer caught a young eagle in the forest, brought it home, and put it with his chickens in their run. He decided to bring it up as a chicken.

A visitor came to the farm a few weeks later and saw the young eagle. 'That isn't a chicken,' he said; 'surely it's an eagle?' 'Yes, you're right,' answered the farmer, 'only it isn't an eagle any more. You see, I've brought it up as a chicken. It will never fly again.' 'I think it will,' said the visitor. 'It's still an eagle after all, and I'm going to help it to fly.' 'Try if you like,' said the farmer, 'but I think you will fail.'

The stranger took the bird out of the chicken-run and held it high in the air. It looked up at the sky, and then looked down again, and finally it jumped back among the chickens. The visitor held the eagle up several times, but each time it looked around and then jumped back to earth. The farmer said, 'You'll never turn that bird back into an eagle.'

Next day at daybreak, the visitor carried the bird to the top of a high hill, and there made it look straight into the rising sun. Suddenly the bird shook itself all over, stretched out its wings, and flew up and away. It had proved that it was an eagle after all.

Then the headmaster would look at his pupils and say, 'Many people think that we Africans are chickens, and I really think we sometimes believe it ourselves. But it's not true! We, too, can be eagles! Let us look into the rising sun and stretch our wings!'

James Aggrey, the headmaster, was born in Ghana. His father, although he sat in the council of the Chief of his tribe, could neither read nor write; but he wanted to give his son a good education. So, when he was 7, James was sent to the Methodist Mission School at Cape Coast.

James did so well that he and a few other boys were invited by one of the masters to come and live in his house, to be trained as teachers. When he was only 15, James Aggrey was put in charge of a small school of about thirty pupils in a village 20 miles away. Aggrey worked so hard and was such a good teacher that a year later he was given

Dr. Aggrey teaching in a village school

Achimota College in Ghana

the chance to move back to Cape Coast and teach in the bigger school there. When he was 23, 7 years later, he became headmaster.

Teaching was not Aggrey's only interest. He also learned to print, and he helped to write and print a local church newspaper. He often used to preach in Sunday School, and he even served in the army for a short time. But in spite of so many things to do, he grew restless. He felt a strong wish to get more education, but at that time there were no colleges in Ghana to which he could go.

The Methodist Church found a place for him at Livingstone, a Negro college in North Carolina, in the southern U.S.A., and Aggrey sailed for America. Few Americans had ever met an educated African before, but Aggrey soon showed them that he was as good as any of his fellow students. After studying for 4 years, he was asked to teach in the college. He married a Negro woman, Rosebud Douglas, and began studying to become a minister. He did not go back to Africa until 22 years later, when he was invited to join a group of American teachers who were studying education in Africa. They visited West, South, and East Africa, and everywhere people listened to Aggrey's wise advice. He always stressed that girls as well as boys should be educated, and that white and black people should work together to improve education in Africa. He used to point to a piano and say, 'You need both white notes and black notes for harmony.'

Then Aggrey returned to Ghana to help set up a big, new school and college at Achimota, just outside Accra, the capital. He set to work with all his old energy, and when the new college opened, the Principal said that Aggrey had done more than any other six men to make it possible. He spent 7 years in Achimota, and then he returned to his family in America. But soon he became ill on a trip to New York and died there.

All Africa mourned the death of this good man, who had worked so hard for the education of Negroes — both girls and boys — and had preached that white men and black men should work together for the good of Africa. James Aggrey had helped the Africans to be free and strong, like the eagle of his story.

18 COCOA FARMING IN GHANA

Cocoa seedling growing in bamboo stem

Cocoa flowers

COCOA FARMING is now one of the most important industries in West Africa, especially in Ghana. Less than 100 years ago, African farmers had never even heard of the cacao tree, from the berries of which drinking cocoa and chocolate can be made. Farmers in South America had been growing cocoa for many generations, and in 1879 the first tiny cacao seedlings were brought to Ghana. Ghana, with its hot, damp climate, heavy rainfall, and fertile soil, is a perfect place for growing cocoa, and soon farmers all over the country were planting their own cocoa crops. There are big plantations owned by international trading companies, but cocoa is also a crop that farmers can raise on their own small farms, for it does not need expensive farm machinery.

A cocoa farmer in Ghana today uses much the same methods of planting, caring for, and harvesting his crop as his grandfather or great-grandfather did many years ago. He can either buy his seedlings or raise them himself on his own land from seed. He plants each seedling in a little pot; he often uses a hollow stalk cut from the stem of a bamboo for this purpose. For several months he tends his seedlings carefully, until they are strong enough to be planted out.

While they are growing, the farmer, perhaps with the help of his neighbours, clears a fresh patch of forest, using knives to cut down the bush and smaller trees, and picks and hoes to dig out all the roots and turn the soil. He leaves the big forest trees standing, for they help to protect the young plants from violent rain-storms and the hot mid-day sun.

Everything must be ready by the time the rainy season comes, for then planting begins. The farmer lays out his seedlings in rows, leaving about 15 feet between the plants. When the trees are fully grown — about 20 feet high — their branches spread out in a wide circle around the tree, so the farmer must leave enough room for them to spread fully. He usually plants vegetables between the rows of trees. It takes 4 years or more before the trees are beginning to bear. During that time, the farmer must keep the land clear of weeds, hoe the soil, prune the young trees, and above all, keep a sharp eye out for signs of disease. One terrible virus disease, called 'swollen-shoot', can kill whole groves of trees. It is probably spread from tree to tree by insects, which feed on infected cocoa trees and then carry the germs in their bodies to healthy trees. This disease cannot be cured, so if a farmer spots the disease on his land, the only thing he can do is cut down and burn all his trees to stop the disease spreading to his neighbour's farm, and then make a new plantation on fresh land.

When the trees are old enough, they begin to produce small, star-shaped flowers directly on the trunk and main branches of the tree. These make hard, ribbed pods, which are green at first but gradually turn to brown and then to yellow. When the pods are yellow, they are ready to be harvested.

At harvest time everyone helps. The men cut the pods off the trees, using hooked knives tied on to the ends of poles. The women and children gather up the fallen pods in their baskets and carry them on their heads to a clearing in the forest. When all the trees have been stripped, and a huge mound of cocoa pods has been built up, everyone gathers in the clearing to shell the beans.

The men form a circle round the heap of pods, and the women sit behind them. The men split open the cocoa pods with their knives and throw them on the ground behind. The women and children pick them up, scrape out as many as sixty beans from each pod, and throw away the pod-shells. When all the pods have been shelled, the beans are spread out on banana leaves and covered with more banana leaves, and left in the forest clearing for several days to mature. During this time the fatty pulp of the bean changes from

Shelling the cocoa pods

a bitter to a pleasant taste. Then the women and children carry the beans in baskets to long tables, which have been set up in the open, and spread them out to dry in the hot sun. Every day they turn the beans over until all the moisture is dried out of them.

When the beans are completely dry, the farmer and his family load them into sacks and carry them to the office of the nearest buyer. They used to carry these sacks on their heads, but now the farmer usually hires a lorry. As soon as he has sold his crop, he can turn to other work on his farm and forget about cocoa for a while. Meanwhile the beans are taken down to the coast by road or rail, loaded into ships, and carried to the chocolate factories of York, Bristol, Birmingham, and other places to be turned into chocolate and drinking cocoa.

The cocoa beans are left to mature in the forest

19 THE TALKING DRUMS OF THE CONGO

Nigerian slit drums

WHEN THE AMERICAN EXPLORER, Henry Stanley, was travelling down the Congo river more than 100 years ago, he was always being surprised at how much the villagers seemed to know about him, even before he arrived in their settlements. Sometimes he would arrive in a village by canoe to find a crowd of Africans waiting for him on the river banks, although he had not sent word that he was coming. There were no telephones or telegraphs in the Congo in those days, and it would have taken hours for a messenger to bring the news through the forest; yet no one seemed surprised that a strange white man had suddenly appeared on the river.

Stanley was not in Africa long, however, before he learned about the 'talking drums'. For hundreds of years, people in parts of Central and West Africa have 'talked' to each other by means of drums, sending news from one village to the next of marriages or births, of wars between neighbouring tribes, the arrival of a traveller, or the presence of dangerous animals. Many villages in the Congo have drums for sending messages to their neighbours, and often there is a special drummer, more skilled than the other villagers in beating out long and complicated sentences.

Two different types of talking drums are used in Africa. The simpler type is made out of a solid log of reddish wood, which has been hollowed out through a long, narrow slit cut in the length of the log, so that the drum looks very much like a long, rounded money-box. The drummer can make high notes by tapping with his drum-sticks on one side of the slit, and low notes by tapping on the other side. The other type of drum, called the skin-top drum, is made by stretching an animal skin over the open end of a hollowed-out log. Skin-top drums are used in pairs — one drum giving a high note, and the other a low note.

But how do the drums really talk? An African in the Congo talks on his drums in very much the same way that he talks in conversation. If you were to listen to two Congo men talking, you would notice that their speech is quite like music: you would hear high notes and low notes, just as if the speakers were singing the words of their sentences. Each word of their language, in fact, has one or more notes, which the speaker 'sings' as he says the word. One word might have two high notes, the next word one high and one low note, and the third word two high notes again, or

Skin-top drums

two low notes. The same words spoken on different notes might mean quite different things. For example, ǎlāmbǎkā b̄oīlī (˘=high; ˉ=low) means in one language 'he watched the river bank'; but if spoken ǎlǎmbǎkǎ b̄oǐlī, it means 'he boiled his mother-in-law'.

The word *songe*, which means 'moon' in a language spoken by the Lokele people in the Congo, has two high notes; and the word *koko*, which means 'fowl', also has two high notes. But when a Lokele drummer hits two high notes on his drum for these words, how does he show that he means *sŏngĕ* and not *kŏkŏ*? Each important word in the drum language has a special little phrase drummed with it to identify it exactly. A drummer who wants to say 'moon' must drum, not just 'moon' but: 'the moon looks down at the earth', or in Lokele: *sŏngĕ lī tăngē lā māngā*. So he beats two high notes for *songe*, a low note for *li*, a high and a low note for *tange*, a low note for *la*, and two low notes for *manga*. When he wants to say *koko* meaning 'fowl', he drums out the phrase: 'the fowl, the little one which says kiokio' — or in Lokele: *koko olongo la bokiokio*. As it takes a great deal of drumming just to say moon or fowl, many of the drum messages are very long indeed.

The message usually begins with a call signal, which may be twenty very fast drum-beats, one after the other. This alerts everyone that a message is about to be sent. Then, if the message is from one particular person to another, the 'drum name' of each person is beaten out before the message is sent. In all villages using talking drums, each boy, as soon as he is old enough to understand the drum language of his tribe, is given a drum name by his father, sometimes in a special drum ceremony. Usually the messages are sent over only a few miles, and are about the simple affairs of ordinary village life — that the fishing is good in a certain river, or that there is to be a tribal meeting. But if the message is very important, it will be passed on from village to village, sometimes over very long distances. For instance, some white travellers once learnt from a drum message that a mail steamer 60 or 70 miles away had been wrecked, only 2 hours after the accident had happened. Drum messages are usually sent only within the tribe, since the drum language of people outside the tribe would be based on a different tribal language. There are, however, some drummers who can speak more than one language, and so can send messages to members of other tribes.

A drum house in the Congo

African villages are very proud of their drums, and take great care of them, sometimes building special huts for them. Some Africans believe that the drums have magical powers, and they use special ceremonies for making and using them. In one Congo village the drum maker may not eat anything for several days before he begins to work, so that his stomach will be hollow like the inside of the drum. There is a story that in one village the people were so pleased with their drum, which was larger than those of any other villages, that they sacrificed the maker and sprinkled his blood over the drum so that he could never make a finer drum for a rival village.

Before white men brought to Africa more modern ways of communicating, almost every boy whose tribe sent messages by drums learned the drum language. They would start, when only 5 or 6 years old, sitting on the ground for hours at a time with two sticks across their knees, practising beating out messages with two small clubs. But, as posts and telegrams and telephones are becoming more common in Africa, the art of drumming is growing rarer.

20 THE BUSHMEN OF THE KALAHARI DESERT

IN EARLIER TIMES most of the people in southern Africa lived by hunting and gathering food, rather than by growing crops and keeping domestic animals, as most Africans do today. So they were always moving from place to place, following the animals they hunted or searching for berries, seeds, or roots. But gradually the African farmers from further north, who needed more land for growing crops and raising cattle, moved down into southern Africa, and drove the hunters and food-gatherers into the lands which were less good for farming — the forests and deserts. The Pygmies are a group of food-gatherers who now live deep in the forests of the Congo Valley. Another group are the Bushmen, who were driven into the Kalahari Desert in the north-west of the Republic of South Africa. Nowadays both the Pygmies and the Bushmen, who may once have been as tall as other Africans, are among the smallest people in the world, perhaps because there was so little food in the forests and deserts where they live.

Bushmen live in small family groups, called bands, consisting of perhaps a dozen people in each band. Each family builds its own simple hut, made of branches which they stick into the ground in a semi-circle and tie together at the top. The main job of the men is to hunt wild animals, such as antelopes or zebras, which they do very skilfully. Sometimes all the men hunt together. For example, during the rainy season when there are swamps in the desert, they make a wide circle round a swamp and move forward together, driving any animals within the circle into the swamp, where they can easily be killed. In the dry season, the Bushmen hunters surround the animals in the same way and drive them towards deep pits which they dig and then disguise with branches. As soon as the animals fall into the pits, the hunters can easily kill them. They also very often kill animals by shooting them with poisoned arrows.

While the men are hunting, the women and children gather food. They search for seeds and berries and use long, pointed digging-sticks with which they dig up those roots which are good for eating. They also hunt for certain kinds of insects which they eat, particularly white ants, or

Bushmen hunting antelopes

A Bushman family. The woman is cracking muhongo nuts for food

termites, and their little white eggs, which are called 'Bushman rice'.

In the desert, where it is dry during most of the year, the biggest problem is to find enough water to drink. The Bushmen can almost always find water where a white man would die of thirst. When everything looks dry and lifeless, the Bushman somehow knows where water is lying underneath the parched, dry land, and he sucks it up to the surface through reeds pushed down into the sand.

When the children grow up, before they are accepted as adult members of the group, they have to go through certain ceremonies and tests. The boys leave their families for a month, while they are taught hunting and other Bushmen skills, learn magic, and pass endurance tests. The girls must stay in their huts, learning which foods may be eaten and which foods the Bushmen may not eat because they will bring evil to the group. When they have completed these ceremonies, the boys and girls are allowed to marry.

Dancing at night round the camp fire. The men dance and the women sing and clap

In many parts of central, eastern, and southern Africa, caves have been found where the ancestors of the Bushmen painted pictures of the animals they hunted — antelopes, zebras, or rhinoceroses. Bits of the ostrich eggshells in which they carried and stored water and paints have also been found. Modern Bushmen are no longer such good artists, but they are still musicians, dancers, and story-tellers. They make pipes from reeds or hollow pieces of wood; they make drums by stretching animal skins across hollow logs; and they make stringed instruments by stretching animal sinews across hollowed-out gourds. In their dances they often imitate the movements of animals, and many of their folk tales are stories about animals and hunting.

Bushmen belong to the past and have very little to do with the modern world; for example, they hardly wear any clothes, as almost all Africans do nowadays. The women wear aprons made of skins, while the men wear a kind of skin loin-cloth. They stitch skins together to use during the day as cloaks and at night as blankets. It seems unlikely that the Bushmen can go on for ever living a life so different from the rest of the world, and some day these little yellow-brown people may disappear altogether from Africa.

21 CHAKA AND THE ZULUS

A Zulu warrior with an assegai and shield

ABOUT 150 YEARS AGO, there were many small tribes of African herdsmen living in Natal, a fertile part of south-eastern Africa. These tribes, who had been in Natal for a long time, lived by raising cattle. But gradually, as their tribes grew larger, they began to run short of good grazing land for their herds. Some of the tribes moved on to the south, looking for fresh pastures, but others stayed on in Natal and fought each other for the good land which was left. In these wars, one of the tribes, the Zulus, fighting under their leader, Chaka, became the most feared warriors in southern Africa, and Chaka built up a powerful kingdom.

Chaka was the son of the Zulu chief. Chaka's mother, Nandi, who was one of the chief's several wives, had a very bad temper. Her son, although he was brave and strong, was hot-tempered too, and he often disobeyed his father. So the chief decided to send away both Nandi and her son, and they were taken in and given shelter by Dingiswayo, the chief of a strong, neighbouring tribe.

Chaka was well treated in his new home, even though he was so proud that the other boys of the tribe disliked him. But Dingiswayo saw that he would make a fine soldier when he grew up, so he trained him to fight in his army. Chaka was so completely fearless and gave so little thought to protecting his own life or those of other people, that even the older warriors began to listen with respect when he spoke at meetings of the tribal council; and soon they made him an officer of the army. In a few years, Chaka's father died, and the Zulus needed a new chief. The Zulu kingdom belonged by rights to one of Chaka's older brothers, but Chaka borrowed a regiment of soldiers from Dingiswayo and conquered the Zulu kingdom.

When he became chief of his own people, Chaka began to try out new ideas for training warriors and fighting battles. The old way of fighting was for each warrior to fight on his own; each soldier would throw his spear at one of the enemy, and then would run forward and fight hand-to-hand with a sword or club. A general had very little control over what his army was doing. But Chaka trained his warriors to stay together in a long line, linking their strong, leather shields for protection; instead of throwing spears they fought the enemy with short, stabbing spears, called assegais. When this great line of warriors got close to the enemy, they easily broke through and scattered the enemy forces.

Chaka decided that he must have a regular army, carefully trained in this new method of warfare and always ready to fight, instead of bands of herdsmen who came together to fight only in war-time and then returned home again. Chaka organized military camps, where all Zulu boys in their teens had to join groups for military training. The most promising boys in each year were taken into the tribe's regular army. The training in the camps was strict and hard. Besides learning to fight, the boys acted as police, messengers, or labourers, and helped to guard the chief's cattle. No warrior was allowed to marry during his army service, and if anyone was caught running away, as many of them tried to do, Chaka had them put to death.

Chaka soon had a highly-trained, powerful army of 40,000 men, and each year he led his army against some neighbouring tribe. No one could stand up against him, and he defeated tribe after tribe, putting the men to death, stealing their cattle, making slaves of the women, and burning the villages to the ground. He extended the Zulu Kingdom over almost the whole of Natal, and then began to raid further down the coast. He was hated and feared over all southern Africa, until his violence and cruelty became too much even for his own people to bear. At last one night he was stabbed and killed in his hut by his brother, Dingaan, and one of the royal attendants. All the Zulus were glad, and Dingaan took Chaka's place as chief of the Zulu people.

The Zulus still live in the northern part of Natal, and no white men are allowed to farm in their country. Life in a Zulu village, or 'kraal', has not changed very much. The groups of beehive-shaped huts are built in a circle around the cattle pens. The men build the huts with a framework of branches, and the women thatch them with grass. The men spend most of their time looking after their cattle, while the women cook the food, carry water, and make pots and baskets for the household. The main changes are that they now have matches, pressure lamps, stoves, and sewing-machines to make their work easier; when their families are ill, they go to modern hospitals instead of to witch-doctors; and most Zulu children now go to school. The boys still play war games, and the men enjoy dressing up in their ostrich-feather head-dresses and dancing the old war-dances on public holidays. But there is no more fighting. Many of the Zulus now live and work in the towns of South Africa, leading the lives of modern townsmen.

A Zulu kraal. A low stockade surrounds the village

22 PAUL KRUGER AND THE AFRIKANERS

The Voortrekkers on the Great Trek

DUTCHMEN FIRST BEGAN to make their homes in South Africa more than 300 years ago, when a Dutch sailor called Jan van Riebeeck built a fortified village at the foot of Table Mountain (where Cape Town is today), and brought a hundred Dutch colonists to man the station. The new station became an important village, where Dutch ships sailing on long trading journeys round the Cape of Good Hope could stop for repairs, fresh food, and drinking water. In the first years, life for the white colonists was often dangerous, for African herdsmen living inland, called Hottentots, used to raid the village and steal their supplies. So the Dutch colonists invited more men to go to the Cape and farm, hoping that they would help defend the settlement. As time went on, more and more farmers arrived, and gradually they drove the Hottentots back from the coast.

In 1806 British soldiers captured Cape Town, and the Dutch farmers and their lands came under the rule of a British governor. Most of the old settlers disliked the new government and also the many English farmers who came to the Cape wanting land. The British and the Dutch also quarrelled over the slaves: the Dutch used Malay or African slaves to work on their farms, and the government passed laws saying that all colonists must give up owning slaves. Many Dutch farmers became so discontented that they decided to take their wives and children, their cattle and goods, and set out in their ox-wagons across the Orange River to search for new lands in the north, away from the British. This journey is called the Great Trek, and the people who went were called the Voortrekkers.

The Great Trek was full of danger and hardship. The trekkers travelled in large family parties with a leader. They took all their belongings in big, canvas-covered wagons, pulled by teams of oxen. There were no roads, and often they had to push the wagons themselves to get them through streams and over mountains. They never could cover more than about 6 miles a day. They were often attacked by bands of African warriors, who tried to take their cattle. The trekkers would defend themselves by quickly tying their wagons together in a circle and shooting at the attackers from behind or under the wagons until the raiders were driven off. Many of the travellers fell ill and died of a terrible fever, called malaria. But they were brave, tough people, and they struggled on. Some of them settled across the Orange River in the Orange Free State, a country of high grassland. Others went on further, over the river Vaal to the Transvaal; and others went further east to Natal (see map p. 58).

When they reached where they meant to settle, they had to clear the bush, build houses, dig fields, and sow crops; and all the time the African tribes, who resented them, were ready to attack and rob them.

Among the trekkers was a boy called Paul Kruger, who was 10 years old when his family set off from the Cape. He grew up on the Great Trek, a strong and sturdy boy, and a good shot with a rifle. But he never had the chance to go to school, and all his life he found it difficult to read and write. His own people read few books except the Bible. They had strict religious ideas, and they believed themselves to be a rather special people of much greater importance in the sight of God than the Africans. Later, when he became a great leader in South Africa, Kruger did not allow Africans an equal place in the country with white men.

The trekkers set up their own governments in their new lands, and spoke their own language, Afrikaans, which had grown out of Dutch. Paul Kruger was 60 years old when the Afrikaners, as these settlers came to be known, chose him as their President in the Transvaal. He was a much-respected and strong ruler, though he was always old-fashioned: he usually wore a quaint, high-buttoned coat and top hat.

In 1886, when Kruger had been President for 3 years, gold was discovered in the Transvaal.

The Kruger monument in Pretoria

Thousands of foreigners — British, French, and Germans — swarmed in, hoping to make their fortunes, and the town of Johannesburg was quickly over-crowded with new settlers. The Afrikaner farmers, although they were glad of the wealth which the gold mines brought to their country, disliked these rough foreigners, whom they called *Uitlanders*, and made them unwelcome. They would not allow them to have any say in how the country was governed, and they kept them out of some trades.

Cecil Rhodes, the Prime Minister of Cape Colony, tried to persuade Kruger and the Afrikaners to treat the miners more fairly (see Chapter 23); but Kruger refused to give in. The Afrikaners and the British grew to dislike each other more and more, until finally in 1899 Kruger declared war on Great Britain. Kruger by then was about 75, too old to fight, so he went to Europe to ask for help in his people's struggle. No help came and, although the Afrikaners fought well and bravely, they were at last defeated by the British army in 1902. Kruger sadly retired to Switzerland, where he died in 1904. His body was taken back to the Transvaal to be buried.

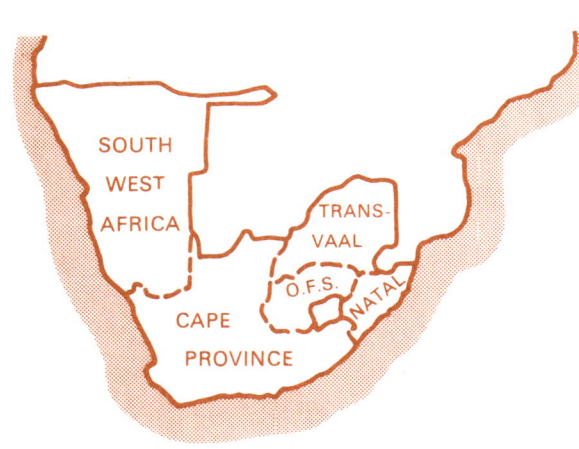

The States of South Africa
(O.F.S. = Orange Free State)

23 CECIL RHODES

CECIL RHODES CAME TO SOUTH AFRICA in 1870 when he was only 17 years old. He left his home in Bishop's Stortford, Hertfordshire, to join his older brother, Herbert, on his cotton farm in Natal. In England Cecil had often been ill, but working hard on the farm in the fresh, dry African climate, he soon grew strong and healthy, a big man, with fair hair and blue eyes. When he was not clearing the bush, planting cotton, or attending to farm accounts, Cecil studied hard, for he was determined to come back to England as soon as he could go to Oxford University.

At this time South Africa was divided into four separate colonies — the Cape Colony, Natal, the Orange Free State, and the Transvaal (see Chapter 22).

The two Rhodes brothers knew that diamonds had been discovered a few years earlier in Kimberley, in the Orange Free State. So in 1871 they decided to try their fortunes at the mines. They sold their farm and set out over hundreds of miles of rough, wild country. They could take very little with them — only one or two picks and spades — for they travelled by ox-wagon; but even then Cecil took a few books to continue his studies.

At Kimberley the brothers bought a small piece of land, and soon they were mining and selling diamonds. As soon as he had made enough money at mining, Cecil sailed for England and went to Oxford. But away from the warm, dry, African climate he soon became ill, and the doctors ordered him to return to Africa. But still Cecil Rhodes meant to take his degree at Oxford. For the next 8 years, he spent part of the year at Oxford and the rest in Africa, until in 1881 he won his degree.

Rhodes was a very good business man and organizer, and he soon saw that all the miners at Kimberley would be better off if everyone worked together, instead of competing with each other. So he persuaded many of them to join with him in a bigger, more efficient company, which he called the De Beers Mining Company. Before long, Rhodes' company controlled almost the whole African diamond industry and was the biggest diamond business in the world. Cecil Rhodes himself became a millionaire. But Rhodes had no use for living grandly; all the time he was in Kimberley, he lived in a little shack with only a few pieces of furniture. He meant to use his wealth for Africa. He believed that Africa could benefit greatly from British ideas of justice and human rights, democracy and fair play. He wanted to unite the small countries in South Africa into one big nation, under the British flag. Once he pointed to a map of Africa and said, 'That is my dream, all British'. In 1880, he stood for the parliament of the Cape Colony, and was elected, for he hoped that way to be able to spread these ideas and encourage the Africans, the Afrikaners (or Boers), and the British to unite under the British flag.

Rhodes was particularly interested in the country in Central Africa, between the Limpopo and Zambezi Rivers and beyond (see Map, p. 11), which was well-suited for white people to settle and farm. Also he knew that there was gold in this part of Africa. So he organized a trading company which he called the British South Africa Company, and this did so well that in 1889 he got permission from the British government not only to trade, but also to rule in all the land north of the Limpopo River. Soon the British South Africa Company was establishing new settlers, running rich gold mines, building railways, and organizing a police force in this new country, which was later called Rhodesia, after its leader. Now, the northern part of it is an independent country, called Zambia.

In 1890 Rhodes became Prime Minister of the Cape Colony. Now was his chance to try to bring the British and Afrikaners, who had always been rivals, to work together for the good of Africa.

An old-time diamond prospector on the Vaal River, Kimberley. The men are washing the soil and sieving it in the large mechanical sieves to pick out any diamonds

He also wanted to give the Africans some share in running their country, and he began to allow them to vote if they could read and write and had a small income. He set up councils for local government in the areas where Africans lived. He described his policy as 'Equal rights for all civilized men'.

But Rhodes could never make friends with Paul Kruger, the leader of the Afrikaners in the Transvaal (see Chapter 22). Rhodes was always an impatient man. He knew he had a weak heart and might die young, and so he was always in a hurry to carry out his plans. He was angry with Kruger because he would not work with him. In 1896 he made a bad mistake. He gave help to a number of British settlers in the Transvaal to revolt against their government, and a hot-headed young friend of Rhodes, called Jameson, led a raid of mounted troops from Rhodesia into the Transvaal. The rebellion was a terrible failure, and Rhodes, who knew he had no right to interfere in the Transvaal, had to give up being Prime Minister. Not long afterwards, there was a war between the English and Boers in South Africa.

Rhodes spent most of the rest of his life in Rhodesia, helping to develop it and bring peace between his British South Africa Company and the Negro Matabele warriors of Rhodesia. He died in 1902, when he was only 49 years old, and was buried in the Matabele country. Later, a fine memorial to him was set up on Table Mountain, near Cape Town. Rhodes left all his great fortune for scholarships for students from English-speaking countries to come and study at Oxford and to take back to their home countries the ideas of freedom and democracy in which he believed so passionately.

24 SOUTH AFRICAN FRUIT FARMING

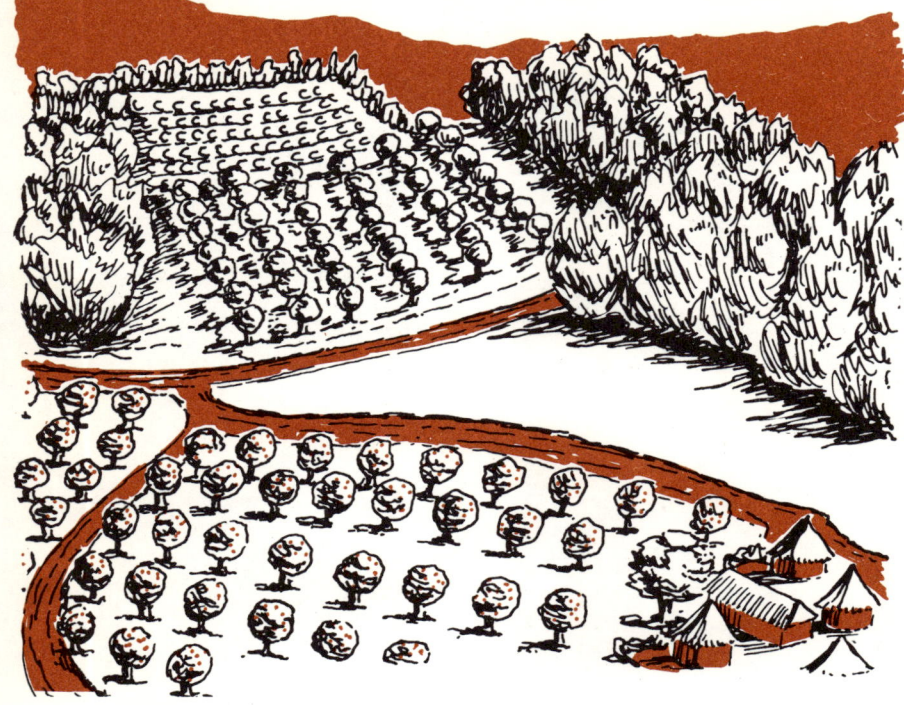

Orange orchards in the Transvaal

THERE IS A GREAT DEAL more sunshine in South Africa than there is in England, and South African farmers can grow splendid fruit of many different kinds. They grow much more than they need for their own use, and so they now send a great deal of fruit and fruit products to Great Britain and other European countries. If you look at the shelves of an English supermarket, you will probably find piles of oranges and apples that have come from South Africa. Many of the tins of sliced peaches, pineapple chunks, or jams will have South African labels; and in the wine section there will be bottle after bottle of South African sherry and brandy and other kinds of wine. As South Africa lies south of the Equator, it is summer there when it is winter in Europe; so people in England can have fresh fruit and vegetables from South Africa during the winter.

The climate varies from one part of South Africa to another, and different kinds of fruit grow well in different parts of the country. Many of the best oranges, for example, come from the Transvaal, where most of the land is higher than the top of the highest mountain in Britain. Because it is so high, although the days are hot and sunny, the nights are cold, and so most of the oranges are grown in the eastern valleys, where the trees are sheltered from wind and frost. The rows of trees, each about 12 feet high, are covered with bright green leaves and orange fruit. There is not enough rain every year, so many farms have reservoirs, made by damming a stream, to provide water for irrigating. The labourers are usually Africans, but the farms belong to white men, often descendants of British settlers, or Afrikaners, descendants of the Voortrekkers, who came from the Cape on the Great Trek (see Chapter 22).

Along the coast in the Eastern Cape Province, the climate is wet and warm for much of the year, and the farmers grow sugar-cane and also many tropical fruits, such as pineapples. Pineapples grow

Growing pineapples

in long rows, on plants which have long, spiky, grey-green leaves coming straight out of the root-base, and a flower spike, rather like a thistle, coming from the middle. This turns into the pineapple. The pineapples to be sent abroad are picked before they are ripe and allowed to ripen on the journey; those to be canned in syrup are left to get fully ripe before being picked and sent to the factory.

Other tropical fruits, such as bananas, avocado pears, mangoes, and melons, grow well in Natal.

Many of the labourers are Zulus from the north, but there are also many Indians, who came to work in South Africa years ago.

The country near Cape Town in the Cape Province is full of rocky hills with fertile valleys, often with streams of rivers running down them. The farmers grow many of the same fruits which people do in Europe — apples and pears, olives, peaches, apricots, and plums. The growers send their fruit to the canning and jam factories in the towns of the Western Cape Province. The most important fruit crop is grapes; millions of bunches of dessert grapes are sent to Britain from here every year, as well as those that come in the form of wine.

The vines grow about 7 or 8 feet tall, and are trained along wires, stretched between posts. The vine leaves, which grow very thick along these trellises, protect the ripening bunches of grapes from being dried up by the hot rays of the sun. Vines growing grapes for wine are cut back to short, stocky little plants, able to resist strong winds and storms. The vines are planted in rows about 6 feet apart, and are cut back to stumps about 2 feet high each March or April, in the South African autumn. About July the farmer sprays them with chemicals to keep them free from disease, and in September or October, in the South African spring, the stumps begin to

A Dutch settler's house, with vineyards

sprout, and then to flower, Gradually the bunches of grapes form, grow bigger, and ripen in the sun, until they are ready to harvest in the new year, at the end of the South African summer. They are taken to big crushing machines, where the juice runs off into tanks and is left to 'ferment'. As the grape juice ferments the sugar in it changes into alcohol. The juice is fermented more for brandy and less for wine. After fermenting, the wine is moved from the tanks into huge, wooden barrels and left to mature until it is right for drinking. The better wines may mature for several years; much of the lighter wine is drunk almost at once.

European farmers have grown fruit at the Cape ever since the first Dutch colonists settled there in the second half of the 17th century. There are still many fine old farm-houses, with white gables and tiled roofs, which look much like farm-houses in Holland. The farm labourers are mostly Cape Coloured people, the descendants of various races who have worked in the Cape Colony in the past, in particular, people who came to South Africa as labourers from Malaya, Hottentots, and Europeans.

Wine vats. Each holds 45,000 gallons

25 JOHANNESBURG

EXCEPT FOR CAIRO IN THE NORTH, Johannesburg is the largest city in Africa. Over a million people live there, of whom more than half are black. It is a modern city, less than 100 years old, a busy, bustling place. As it is the chief business centre of South Africa, the middle of the city has tall, modern office blocks, hotels, apartment houses, and fine, big shops filled with things to buy. It is a rich, prosperous city, and most of the people, both white and black, are well-dressed. It is not surprising that Johannesburg should be rich, for it is 'built on gold' — that is to say, it is the centre of South Africa's gold-mining industry, and more than half of all the gold produced today comes from Africa.

Johannesburg stands in the middle of the Transvaal (see map p. 51) on a high ridge of land called in Afrikaans the Witwatersrand (Ridge of White Waters), or just the Rand. It is 6,000 feet above sea level, so the nights are always cool and in winter often very cold. The days are pleasantly warm for there is a great deal of sunshine. In fact, the climate is very good and very healthy, for the winters are dry and there is not too much rain in the summer.

Less than 100 years ago there was no city on the Rand at all, only villages and herds of cattle and flocks of sheep grazing on the dry grassland. Then, in 1886, some mining engineers found outcrops of gold on the Rand, and before long thousands of people were rushing there from all over the world in the hope of making their fortunes. Johannesburg began as a temporary camping place for the gold-seekers' ox-drawn covered wagons. But not much of the gold on the Rand was close to the surface, which miners could reach on their own with very simple tools, and this was soon exhausted. There was plenty of gold, but it was buried deep in the rock, perhaps a mile underground, and only big companies able to afford expensive machinery could dig it out. So the gold-mining industry was carried on by companies who employed a great many Africans as workers.

As the gold-mining increased, so did Johannesburg grow. It was named after Johannes Rissik, the chief official in the Transvaal. All round it, stretching for 40 miles or more east and west, were gold mines. The miners brought up quantities of rock and crushed it to extract the gold; then it was dumped in high white mounds all over the country, even close into the city, and these today make a strange, untidy background to the modern city.

Johannesburg now has many other industries besides gold. Among other things, the factories make machinery for mining, both for South Africa and other countries. Also it is an important meeting place for roads, railways, and air-routes. In Johannesburg the white and black people do not live together, but in separate suburbs of the city. This is because the South African government thinks that the different kinds of people in the country should not mix up

Gold-miners. Their helmets have battery-supplied lamps

Gold-mining dumps on the outskirts of Johannesburg

but should progress separately. It has passed laws about this separation — called 'Apartheid' in Afrikaans—and one law says that black and white people must live in different areas. There are many more rich white citizens than black, and the white suburbs are far more beautiful, with some fine houses in their own large gardens. The black people used to live in dirty slums full of old shacks, but these are gradually being cleared and decent housing estates built instead. Even so, many of South Africa's black people, and also some of the whites, dislike this separation, feeling that it is inconvenient, often unfair, and not very natural.

Other big industrial towns have grown up on the Rand, which is the biggest industrial centre in Africa. But many of these towns are more attractive to look at than industrial towns in Europe, for there are open places and parks, the main streets are lined with trees, and there are often fine suburbs for the wealthy.

Most of the African workers in the gold mines do not come from Johannesburg but from other parts of South Africa, or from nearby African countries. They sign on to work as miners for a year or more; they have to leave their families at home, and while they are working they live in barracks near the mines. They have to work very hard underground, cutting and blasting the rock and bringing it to the surface. But hard and restricted as their conditions of life are, they earn good money, and after 2 or 3 years many of them are able to take savings back to their distant families.

26 THE EUROPEANS IN AFRICA

AFTER THE PORTUGUESE SAILORS had explored down the coast of Africa some 500 years ago, and Vasco da Gama had finally sailed round the Cape of Good Hope (see Chapter 13), the Portuguese, and, later, the Spanish, Dutch, French, and British, set up trading posts, with forts to protect them, all round the African coast. But for hundreds of years they hardly ventured inland at all, except in South Africa where European farmers, especially Dutch, had been settling and gradually pushing out further and further since about 1660.

The Europeans were interested in Africa only for trade, and far the most important trade was slaves. The traders did not have to go inland to capture slaves, for the African chiefs themselves captured the slaves in their wars with each other, and they delivered the wretched slaves to the European trading posts or ships (see Chapter 14). The French slave traders obtained their slaves mainly from Senegal (see Chapter 16); the British obtained theirs from the coasts of what are now Ghana and Nigeria; and the Portuguese from further south — Angola on the west coast and Mozambique on the east. So, apart from a very few explorations such as Mungo Park's journeys to the river Niger, Europeans knew almost nothing about Central Africa (see Map p. 11).

Then several things happened to change this. During the late 18th and early 19th centuries people began to realize how wicked the slave trade was, and laws were passed to stop it. By 1833 slavery was altogether stopped in any part of the British Empire; it went on in the southern states of America until 1865; but it lasted much longer in the East (see Chapter 32). As the slave trade died out, merchants sought other kinds of trade, and explorers began to make expeditions into Africa to find out what it was like. After the explorers came missionaries. During Queen Victoria's reign many people in Britain gave large sums of money to their churches to send missionaries to Africa to teach them about Christianity and to help them in many other ways, and the Roman Catholic churches also sent many missionaries. The missionaries settled among the Africans and not only built churches but also schools and hospitals.

One of the most important of these medical missionaries was David Livingstone, whose story is told in Book 2 of this series. He was an explorer as well as a missionary (see Chapter 29), and he did everything he could to interest people at home in the people of Africa, to get more helpers to come to Africa, and to get the British government to stop slavery. The European governments encouraged the explorers and missionaries, and also the trading companies which began to work along the river Niger and in central and eastern Africa; but they hesitated to interfere in Africa, and would not, for example, do anything to stop the African chiefs selling slaves to Arab traders.

Then, about 100 years ago, this changed quite suddenly. The rulers of Belgium and Germany needed new lands overseas in which Belgians and

Africa in 1914

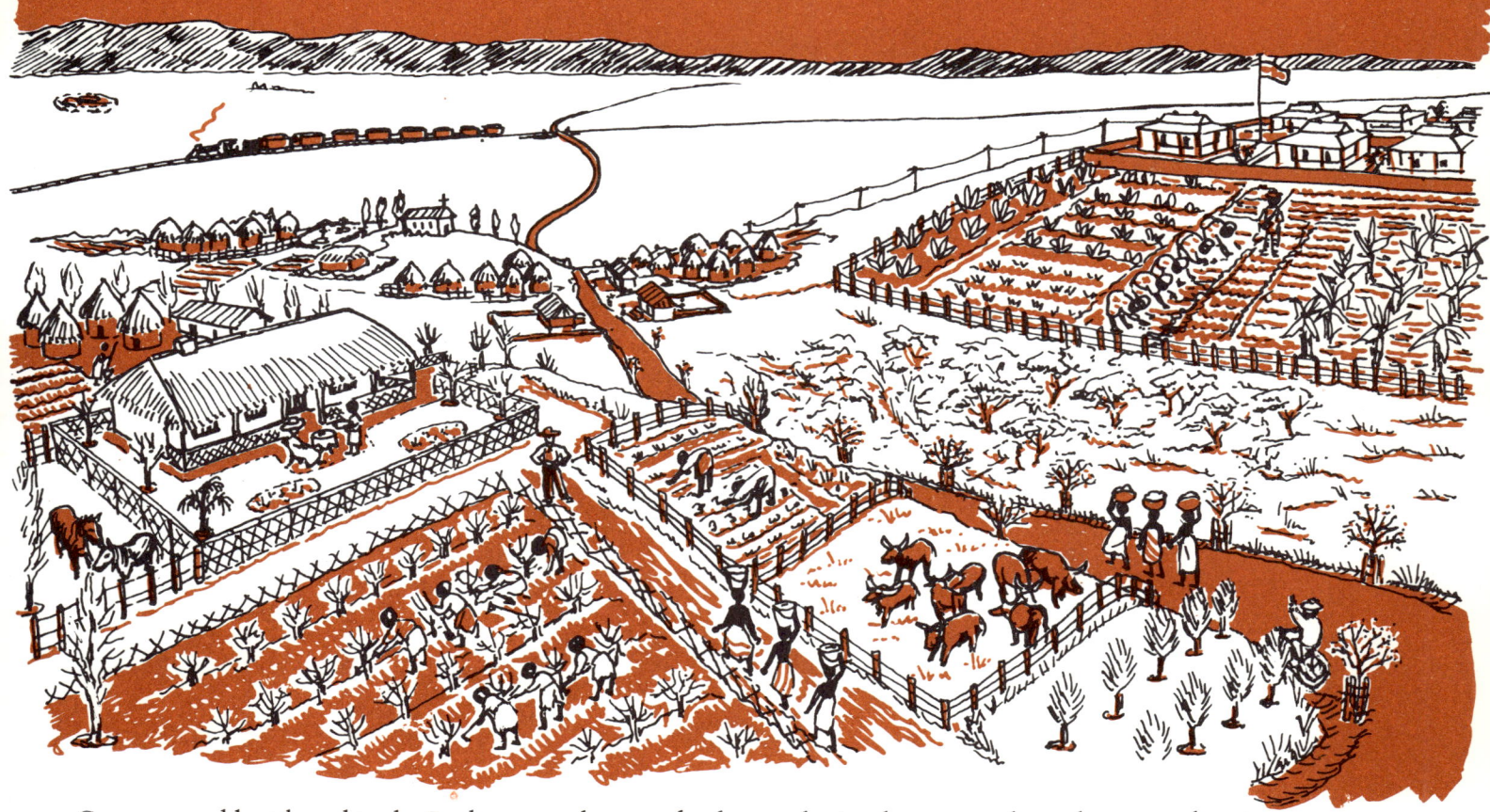

A tea plantation about 1890. The workers are African, many of them prisoners from the fort at the back

Germans could settle and trade. So they started to persuade the African chiefs to put themselves under their protection. Very soon Great Britain and France, and later Italy, realized that, if they were not active, they would lose their opportunity. In fact, the European countries all started to 'scramble' for lands in Africa, and in the years from 1880 to 1900 almost the whole of Africa was divided up between them. Only Ethiopia (see Chapter 43) and the small country of Liberia on the west coast remained independent countries. Liberia had been established early in the 19th century by the Americans as a country to which freed slaves from America could return and be independent.

The map shows how Africa was divided up among European countries by 1914, the year the First World War broke out. What, in fact, had happened was that each European country had advanced inland from its original coastal trading stations. The French, starting from Senegal, had occupied a large part of the north-west; the Portuguese controlled Angola in the south-west and Mozambique in the south-east; the Belgians controlled the lands of the Congo; the Germans took lands mostly in the east and south-west; the British advanced north and east from the west coast, and Rhodes' British South Africa Company moved northwards from Cape Colony.

The Europeans did much good in Africa. They brought slavery to an end and stopped the endless fighting between tribes. They built roads and railways, and, later, airports. They set up schools and hospitals, and they built modern towns and improved agriculture. In fact, they brought Africa in touch with the modern world. The Africans liked these things, but they soon grew to hate being treated as inferior people and being governed by foreign rulers. Particularly as many of them became more educated, they longed to rule their own countries themselves.

Most European governments sympathized with this feeling and saw that the time had now come when they should no longer rule people against their own wish. So, after the Second World War, one African country after another demanded and was granted its independence. In the 9 years between 1957 and 1966 almost all the European colonies of 1914 became independent countries (see Map p. 10).

27 TSETSE FLIES OF TROPICAL AFRICA

THE EQUATOR RUNS ACROSS THE CENTRE of Africa through the lands of the Congo river and the region of the great lakes. Much of this country is covered with tropical forests, and north and south of the forests lie hot grasslands called the savanna. These grasslands would be suitable for grazing herds of the kinds of cattle which can live in hot countries, were it not for the tsetse flies. The tsetse flies do so much harm that many scientists spend all their time studying them to try to find out what is the best way of getting rid of them.

Tsetse flies are not very exciting to look at. They are rather bigger than ordinary house flies, and are grey or dark-brown in colour. They have piercing and sucking organs sticking out from the front of their heads, for they feed by piercing the skin and sucking the blood of other animals. They attack many of the wild animals of the savanna, especially wart-hogs, elephants, buffaloes, and some kinds of antelopes. They also attack domestic cattle. They seem to prefer animals with dark skins and usually do not bite zebras with their white stripes or the lighter coloured antelopes. Some kinds particularly favour the blood of man.

The reason why they are so dangerous is not because of their bite, but because they carry a fatal disease called sleeping sickness, and pass it on to whatever animal or human they bite. The tiny germs of this disease, called trypanosomes, live in the blood of animals. They do no harm in the blood of most wild animals, such as wart-hogs or antelopes. But, when a tsetse fly bites and sucks the blood of an antelope, for example, it sucks in some of the sleeping sickness trypanosomes, and then injects them into the blood of the next animal it bites. If this should be a human being or a domestic cow or horse or dog, the victim falls ill of the sleeping sickness disease.

Today it is possible to cure people who get the disease, but cattle usually waste away and die. Therefore it has not been possible for Africans

Typical tsetse-fly country. The cattle here have been inoculated and carry the inoculation mark

with herds of cattle to settle in those parts of Africa where there are tsetse flies, and it is very important for the future of Africa to find out how to get rid of them.

Tsetse flies need moisture, warmth, and shade in order to breed. They find this best in the damp, hot, tropical forests. So in many parts of Africa it was thought that if the forests were cleared and all the trees in the grasslands cut down, the flies would not be able to breed, and so die out. But it is impossible to clear all the forests, and also land needs trees to keep it fertile and to prevent it from being washed away by heavy rain. Even in the places where the forests were cleared, the tsetse flies continued to breed in any little pockets of forest that were left.

Then scientists thought that if they killed all the wild animals on which the flies fed and which carried the trypanosomes in their blood, they might destroy the disease; and so thousands of animals were killed. But neither destroying the animals nor destroying the forests was a practical or desirable thing to do. So now scientists are trying to find a form of inoculation to prevent people or animals getting the disease, just as dogs are prevented from getting distemper, or humans, smallpox. Already cattle can be inoculated so that they are safe from the disease for several months, and can graze in tsetse country for part of the year. Also insecticides such as DDT are some use in killing the flies, but this is very expensive.

Another suggestion is to farm animals which do not suffer from the disease, such as antelopes, instead of trying to farm cattle in tsetse country. The Africans need more meat, but they might eat venison instead of beef.

Hole punched in ear of cows to show that they have been inoculated

28 ZIMBABWE

Fort Victoria

Stone bird from Zimbabwe

IN THE SOUTHERN PART OF RHODESIA, on the road running from Johannesburg to Salisbury, the capital of Rhodesia, there is a small town called Fort Victoria. This town is growing more important now because a big dam has been built a few miles away. The reservoir, called Lake Kyle, made by the dam, has provided water to irrigate land which used to be dry and useless. Now there are plantations of sugar-cane and oranges and lemons. Rhodesians, both white and black, are proud of this area: the white people remember that Fort Victoria was the first European town — the beginning of modern Rhodesia; the black people remember that near here was Zimbabwe, the centre of one of the greatest African kingdoms of the old days.

About 80 years ago Cecil Rhodes (see Chapter 23) was given permission by the British Government to start a colony with lands north-east of South Africa. The first group of settlers and their families moved north in their covered ox-wagons, guided by a famous hunter called F. C. Selous. They hauled their wagons slowly through ranges of hills, taking care to keep out of the way of the fierce Matabele tribes. Every night, when they camped, they had to get watchmen to watch against surprise attacks from Africans or, indeed, from wild animals. At last they got through the hills and dropped down to a pleasant stretch of flat land, where they decided to stop and build a settlement. The new colony was called Rhodesia after Rhodes, and this first settlement was called after Queen Victoria. Every night a bell was rung at 9 o'clock to warn the settlers to lock up their houses and post guards for the night, and this bell is still rung from a tower in the fort in memory of these early days.

Some years before the farmers settled round Fort Victoria, hunters such as Selous were exploring the country, and miners were looking for gold. An ivory-hunter called Adam Renders, making his way through thick bush, suddenly came on the ruins of great granite stone walls. The ruins were quite deserted and half grown over with trees and bushes. No-one appeared to be living anywhere near, and he could find no clue to show what the ruins had been.

All the ruins have now been carefully cleared, and Great Zimbabwe, as it is called, has been thoroughly explored by experts to find out who had once lived there. Zimbabwe consists of a strong, stone fortress built on a rocky hill; a number of smaller buildings in the valley below; and beyond them a strange, cone-shaped tower surrounded by huge stone walls, at places as high as 30 feet and 14 to 16 feet wide. The walls are made of huge blocks of granite laid one on top of another, and fitted so well that they need no mortar to hold them together.

In the Middle Ages, the people of Zimbabwe mined a great deal of gold, sold it to merchants, and so became rich. Their king, who was called the Monomatapa, had a fine city built, where he lived in pomp and state. Ornaments and pottery from as far away as China have been found in the city, and these must have been brought to Zimbabwe by merchants in exchange for gold.

About 400 years ago, when the Portuguese had found their way round the Cape of Good Hope, they began to explore up the river Zambezi from the coast. There, near the river, living in a city made of mud and thatch, they met the reigning Monomatapa, who had been driven from Zimbabwe by more powerful people called the Rozwi. The Monomatapa and his people had lost most of their old grandeur and wealth, and had been deserted by many of their followers.

The Rozwi also mined gold and exchanged their gold for ornaments, cloth, and pottery. They were even better builders than the Monomatapa's people, and it was they who built the cone-shaped tower and the huge stone walls. The Rozwi people continued to live round Zimbabwe until about 150 years ago, when they, also, were attacked and driven out by yet stronger fighters, people who were moving away from Natal to escape the wars of Chaka (see Chapter 21).

When the ivory-hunter, Adam Renders, found Zimbabwe in the year 1868, it must have been lying completely deserted for about 40 years. Now, people from all over the world go to visit it.

Zimbabwe. The tower and enclosure seen from the fortress

29 THE ZAMBEZI RIVER

Fish traps in the Zambezi swamps

SINCE ANCIENT TIMES, Arab traders had been sailing their big dhows, with great three-cornered sails, across the Indian Ocean to the mouth of the Zambezi river on the east coast of Africa. The first European to discover the river was Vasco da Gama, and he saw the Arab traders loading up cargoes of ivory, gold, and slaves. He carried this news back to Portugal. Soon other Portuguese adventurers and traders came, and they explored as far up the river as boats could be sailed. When they reached rapids through which no boat could pass, they built a trading settlement and fort, called Tete.

The first person to explore the whole river was the Scottish medical missionary David Livingstone (see Book 2). He discovered that the Zambezi flows from highlands not so far from the west coast, right across tropical Africa to the east coast, a distance of more than 1700 miles.

The Zambezi rises in swamps in the highlands, from which many streams run north and west to the Atlantic, and others flow south-eastwards, join the Zambezi, and reach the Indian Ocean. The Africans who live round these swamps are fishermen. They catch fish by putting basket-work traps in narrow parts of the streams. Instead of eating the fish fresh, they cut it up and lay it out to dry in the sun. This makes it smell and taste much stronger, which they prefer.

The river runs in a clear fast-flowing stream down through forests and hills until it reaches the plains. Then it widens out and flows more slowly through fertile country, where the African farmers live in little villages near its banks and grow good crops of maize, millet, and vegetables.

Hippos in the Zambezi

But, after heavy rain in the hills, the river sometimes floods and sweeps all their crops away. Also huge hippopotamuses come up from the river at night and eat and trample down the crops just as the farmers are going to harvest them. The farmers make chains of bonfires along the river bank to scare the hippos away, and watchmen sit up all night on raised platforms, well out of the way of crocodiles, and rattle tin cans to frighten the hippos. Sometimes a herd of elephants, coming to the river to drink, will trample down both crops and village huts.

When the river reaches western Zambia, it flows for about 200 miles through a great plain where the Barotse tribes live. They build their homes on higher pieces of ground or they make grass huts on tall wooden poles well above the level of the floods. They are boatmen, and they make canoes hollowed out of tree-trunks, either single ones or big enough to take a dozen men, and they propel them with huge paddles or long poles. When the floods go down in June, they plant their crops in the mud and harvest them before the river rises again.

All along the Zambezi valley there are many kinds of wild animals. There are flamingoes and pelicans and snake-birds (see Chapter 7) and flocks of wild geese and ducks and brilliantly-coloured kingfishers. In the river, as well as crocodiles, there are electric catfish which stun their prey with an electric shock, and 'squeakers' with poisoned spines, and fierce tiger-fish. Many kinds of antelopes, elephants, leopards, and other wild animals come down to the river to drink.

When the river is more than a mile wide, it suddenly drops over a great cliff and falls 350 feet down into a narrow zig-zag gorge below, throwing up huge clouds of spray. When Livingstone first saw this great waterfall, which the Africans call *Mosioa-tunya* or 'Smoke thunders', he named it the Victoria Falls, and the modern town nearby is named after Livingstone himself. Just below the Falls, a road and railway bridge was built over the gorge in 1905. There are only three bridges across the whole Zambezi from source to mouth — two carrying a railway and one only a road. Otherwise people have to cross the river by ferry boat, or stay one side or the other.

The Karoba Dam

Below the Falls the river runs through wild country where many animals, but few people, live because of the tsetse flies (see Chapter 27). After about 200 miles the river passes through a deep gorge with rocky cliffs on either side. Here, in 1960, a great dam, called the Kariba Dam, was built across the gorge to hold back the water. So much water was held back that now there is a huge man-made lake, about 170 miles long. The power of the water is used to make electricity for Rhodesia and Zambia. When the lake was made, all the animals in the valley which was going to be flooded had to be caught and driven or carried away so that they should not be drowned, and all the villages in the valley had to be rebuilt elsewhere. The road which runs across the Kariba Dam makes a fourth way to cross the river.

After another 100 miles or so, the Zambezi flows into Mozambique and runs through low, very hot country where people grow sugar-cane and cotton. Then it reaches Tete, the old Portuguese town, to which, in old days, paddle-steamers used to bring cargo and passengers up from the coast. When it is near the coast, the river divides into several smaller streams, which make their way through coconut palms to the sea.

Barotse boatmen

30 THE HARE AND THE PUMPKINS

THIS STORY IS TOLD IN MALAWI. In African animal stories, the clever Hare is a favourite character, who often comes off best by outwitting the bigger and stronger animals. In many ways he is like the Brer Rabbit of American stories. There is a Tibetan story of how the Hare outwits the Tiger (see Book 9).

One evening the animals were standing at the forest edge, talking about food. 'I get so tired of leaves and grass,' said Elephant. 'I wish I could find something more interesting to eat.' 'Why don't you grow some pumpkins?' asked Hare. 'They're very good to eat, and not difficult to grow. I shall be planting some seeds tomorrow. If you like you can come and watch and see how it's done.' 'Yes, I will,' said Elephant.

The next day Hare was hard at work before dawn. He had already hoed his field and pulled out the weeds some days before. Now he scraped up the earth into little mounds a few feet apart, hollowed out holes in the mounds, and watered them; then he planted a seed in each. Late in the morning, when he had nearly finished, Elephant appeared.

For a while Elephant stood and watched. 'That doesn't look too difficult,' he said. 'I think I should like to grow some pumpkins. Will you give me some of your seeds?' Now Hare did not have much seed to spare, but he didn't want to offend Elephant. 'All right,' he said, 'I'll give you some of my seed to start you off. Don't forget to hoe the land first and get rid of the weeds.' 'I'm afraid I've lost my hoe,' Elephant replied. 'Would you mind lending me yours?' Hare hated lending his hoe to anyone, but he still didn't want to make an enemy of Elephant, so he reluctantly agreed. 'Thank you,' said Elephant, 'that's very kind of you. Now I wonder if you'd come over to my field tomorrow and help me with a little digging? My back gets so stiff these days.' This was too much for Hare. 'No, I won't,' he said. 'I'm not going to do everything for you. But I'll come over in a week or so and see how you're getting on.'

When Hare visited Elephant's field about 10 days later, there was no one about. Most of the field was still covered with weeds, and only some miserable little mounds of earth here and there showed where a few seeds had been planted. The hoe was lying under a bush where it had been dropped. Hare picked up his hoe and went home, forgetting all about Elephant.

Weeks passed, and Hare's crop of pumpkins began to ripen. He was going to have a wonderful harvest. There were two enormous pumpkins near the middle of the field that were bigger than he had ever grown before. When the first of them was ready to eat, Hare invited all his friends to come and celebrate with a feast.

On the morning of the party, he went down early to his field to pick the pumpkin, for it would take a long time to cook. He walked

Hare planting his pumpkin seeds

Hare climbs into his pumpkin

happily to the middle of the field, but then he had a very unpleasant surprise. All he found on the plant was a broken stalk, and the precious pumpkin had been stolen.

Hare's party was very sad, and most of the conversation was about the theft. Everyone thought that the thief must have been Elephant. All the animals were afraid that Elephant would steal the rest of the good pumpkins as well, so Hare put his wits to work on a plan to save the rest of his crop.

He did nothing until the other big pumpkin was ripe and ready to eat. Then with his knife he cut a hole in its underside, and scraped out all the inside of the pumpkin. Then, as soon as it was dark, he went down to the field with his spear and drum and climbed through the hole into the pumpkin. Then he settled down and waited.

The night was so still that Hare was sure he would hear anyone coming, while he was still quite far away. He listened very hard, but he heard no sound. It was cosy and warm inside the pumpkin, and before long Hare fell asleep. When he suddenly woke up in the night, he could not make out what was happening; the world seemed to be swinging about. Then he caught a glimpse of moonlight on a white tusk, and then everything went dark. Hare realized that Elephant had swallowed the pumpkin with himself inside.

Elephant was feeling very contented. The second pumpkin had looked as good as the first, and he was pleased to be teaching a good lesson to that selfish neighbour, who had refused help with a little digging. Then suddenly a drum started beating, very close by. 'They're after me,' thought Elephant, and he hurried off toward the forest, not stopping to rest until he had reached the trees.

But the drum started beating again, and it sounded no further away than before. What was happening? Elephant was so alarmed that he began to run, and he kept on running for 4 miles. At last he stopped and leaned, panting, against a tree. Immediately the drum began again, just as loud as ever. Elephant fled in terror, his great sides heaving, and he ran and ran for mile after mile until he dropped exhausted to the ground.

Then Hare crawled out of his pumpkin and made his way through Elephant's inside and out of his mouth. Then he slid down a tusk to the ground. For a moment he thought of saying a few forceful words to Elephant. But he thought better of it, and with the drum in his hand and the spear under his arm, Hare set off for home.

Hare slides down Elephant's tusk

31 KILWA

Arab dhows sailing to Mombasa harbour

IF PEOPLE LIVING IN MOMBASA in Kenya or Dar es Salaam in Tanzania want a new carpet or some tiles for their house, they usually wait until early in the New Year when the merchants from Persia or India arrive, bringing goods from the east. For as long as 2000 years these merchants, mainly Arabs, have been sailing their dhows with great triangular-shaped sails from Asia to the harbours in eastern Africa. They sail with the monsoon winds which blow steadily south-westwards from November to March. Then, when the monsoon changes and in April and May blows north-eastwards, the dhows load up with mangrove poles, coconuts, and in old days with gold, ivory, and slaves, and sail away again to the north. We can guess what these early voyages were like from the stories of Sinbad the Sailor, for he visited the country of the black men and took on a cargo of coconuts to carry to Baghdad.

Today, the trade of these sailing-ships is slowly dying out, for now big merchant ships are taking their place. But in the Middle Ages, peoples of the East African coast traded with all the countries of the Indian Ocean and even as far as China. The greatest trading town of all was Kilwa, which stands on an island about 160 miles south of the modern city of Dar es Salaam. Kilwa grew important because between the island and the mainland there is a magnificent sheltered harbour, and because the trading ships could get supplies of good drinking water from the mainland. So the ships used Kilwa as a port of call from early times.

The early inhabitants of Kilwa were Negroes who moved down to the sea from lands near Lake Victoria. The Arab traders brought with them their Moslem religion, and some of them settled on the coast and married African wives. Gradually there grew up a language which we call Swahili, which was mostly Bantu African and partly Arabic, and which is now the main African language of East Africa.

The first ruler of Kilwa about whom we know anything was called Ali bin al-Hasan. He came to Kilwa from the north, probably from what is now Somalia, about the year 1200, and he made the first coins ever used in East Africa. Kilwa was by then a Moslem town with several mosques built of coral rock. Ali bin al-Hasan's successors made Kilwa more and more wealthy. The gold from Zimbabwe in Rhodesia (see Chapter 28) was brought to the Kilwa markets, and with the profits from gold the Kilwa rulers bought luxuries, such as beautiful Chinese porcelain, and built fine new buildings in stone.

The finest and largest building was the ruler's palace called Husuni Kubwa, which means Big Fort. It was built on high land above the town and spread over 2 acres, with more than 100 rooms arranged in squares round sunken courtyards. There was a bathing pool, and store-rooms for the palace treasure, and in the centre, reached by a flight of steps, was a lofty room where the ruler, no doubt, received his visitors. To the north was a broad flight of steps leading down to the sea. In this splendid palace the ruler must have lived in grandeur and state.

When the Portuguese reached Kilwa about 1500, they were astonished to find such a city in Africa. 'In this land,' wrote one of them, 'there are rich merchants and much gold and silver and amber and musk and pearls. The people wear clothes of fine cotton and silk and many beautiful ornaments — and they are black men.'

But the glory of Kilwa came to an end, as happened with most of the great kingdoms in different parts of Africa. The rulers quarrelled among themselves, and the Portuguese took control of the gold trade. Then bands of cannibal warriors came from the mainland, attacked the city, and slew the people. For a time, about 150 years ago, Kilwa was important as a port for the slave trade; but then a new trading centre was built on the mainland, and Kilwa fell into ruins. Now it is nothing more than a small fishing village.

Kilwa as it now looks

32 IVORY AND SLAVES IN EAST AFRICA

An Arab caravan with African porters

WHEN VASCO DA GAMA first reached the coast of East Africa in 1498, he saw Arab merchants loading their ships with ivory and slaves at the mouth of the Zambezi river, and, as we read in the last chapter, Kilwa grew rich by selling ivory and slaves to the Arab traders. Today, slavery has been stopped altogether, and the elephants which live on the grasslands of eastern Africa are protected by law. No one is allowed to shoot them without an expensive licence, and even then, only a few may be killed.

Merchants in old days wanted the ivory tusks of elephants to sell in the markets from Rome to China, for making jewellery and ornaments. The African hunters used to kill the elephants either by shooting them with poisoned arrows or by digging deep pits, disguising them with branches, and then driving the elephants into them. Then they cut out the ivory tusks and sent them to the market towns such as Kilwa. Slaves also were wanted as household servants; they were sometimes called 'black ivory'. The African chiefs, when they went to war with each other, used to capture prisoners and send them down to the coast to sell to the merchants. Egyptians and Arabs had been coming down the coast of East Africa since the days before the birth of Christ in search of ivory and slaves.

About 150 years ago, when the slave trade in West Africa was gradually being stopped (see Chapter 14), it was increasing in the east. Slaves were wanted as labourers in the new sugar plantations, being started in the islands of the Indian Ocean, and more and more were wanted. Then, in 1840, the Arab Sultan of Oman, in Arabia, settled in the big island of Zanzibar and made plantations of cloves and coconuts. He wanted slaves to work these plantations. An enormous slave market grew up in Zanzibar, and thousands of men, women, and children were brought every year by the cruel and greedy traders and were put up for sale in the big open space in Zanzibar town, where the cathedral now stands.

Both ivory and slaves were brought from inland along the main trade routes through Uganda and Kenya and Tanzania and Malawi to the coast, but still the traders wanted more ivory and more slaves. So the Arabs began to go inland to find them for themselves. They went in big, armed, caravan parties (see Chapter 34), and they bribed the African chiefs with cloth and guns and other goods to supply them with slaves. The chiefs used the guns for raiding other tribes in order to seize men, women, and children and sell them to the Arabs. And so fighting and misery spread.

In some parts, especially near Lake Malawi, whole districts were emptied of people, and the villages and crops were destroyed. When David Livingstone explored through this country in 1866, this was the misery he saw. It made him so angry that he called the slave trade 'the open sore of the world', and he did all he could to make other people understand how cruel and wicked it

Zanzibar as it is today

was. While Livingstone and other people were trying to bring slavery to an end, the Arab caravans reached right into the Congo, where some of the finest ivory was to be found. Gradually, however, people became disgusted with so much cruelty. About 1867, the Sultan of Zanzibar was persuaded to close the great slave markets in his country. Also, as Europeans spread over East Africa (see Chapter 26), they put an end to much of the fighting between African tribes. By about 1900, the last of the African slaves had been freed.

There are still many Arabs living along the East African coast, and some still trade in ivory. In 1964, however, in Zanzibar, the people rose in revolt against the Arab Sultan and drove him out and killed many of the Arab settlers. Now, Zanzibar has joined with Tanganyika to form the new African country of Tanzania.

33 THE MAN-EATERS OF TSAVO

THE COUNTRY OF UGANDA lies some 500 miles or more inland from the East African coast, and the early British officials and missionaries working there were in difficulties because it took so long for supplies to reach them. There was no railway nor proper road, and everything had to be carried on the heads of African porters. In these conditions the British could not develop the country properly, nor could they stop the slave trade, which still went on in spite of the law.

In 1895, the British government decided to build a railway from Mombasa on the coast into Uganda. After about 130 miles of railway had been built, the line met the river Tsavo, and an engineer, Lt. Col. J. H. Patterson, was sent to build a bridge. Patterson found the camp on the river noisy with the shouts of the workmen, the hammering of metal, and the blast of explosives. Several thousand workmen were living in camps of tents, mostly Indians who had been brought over to do the building work, but also about 1400 African porters.

After Patterson had been at Tsavo camp for only a few days, he was told one morning that two Indian workers had disappeared from their tent in the night, and that they must have been taken by man-eating lions. Patterson thought it more likely that there had been a quarrel, and that the two Indians had been killed and secretly buried, for lions do not normally attack human beings. Old lions, which have become too slow to hunt game, do sometimes take to eating human flesh, and then they can be very cunning and dangerous.

But three weeks later, an Indian foreman disappeared from his tent during the night, and a trail of paw marks led away into the bush. By following the trail, Patterson found the remains of the foreman's body and traces of two lions. He knew that, if work on the railway was to go on smoothly, he must kill the lions or at least drive them out of the area. He did not realize what a difficult job he had undertaken.

That evening, armed with a rifle and shot-gun, he climbed into a tree overlooking the tent where the lions had last attacked. Several Africans sat up with him. Soon they heard the roaring of the lions coming gradually nearer. Then it stopped, as it always does when lions begin to stalk their prey. For almost two hours there was silence; then suddenly screams came from another camp half a mile away.

For weeks Patterson sat up with his rifle every night, but always, while he watched in one camp,

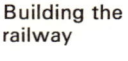
Building the railway

the lions attacked in another. They seemed to know where Patterson would be hiding, and night after night they dragged off a victim into the bush. The workers began to believe that the lions had magic powers.

One night Patterson and the medical officer, Dr. Brock, hid in a supply wagon on the railway line. They did not know that the lions were watching and had chosen them as the night's prey. But when one of the lions suddenly leapt out of the darkness at them, they were ready for it and fired. The shots missed, but the flash and noise of the rifles frightened the man-eaters off, and for some time they did not attack. Then one night the Tsavo camps were again awakened by screams. The man-eaters were back. The workers tried to protect themselves by building strong, brushwood fences around their tents and lighting great fires at night. But the lions always managed to get through the fences; they disregarded the fires, and had become so bold that they did not even bother to carry their victims away before devouring them.

At last the workers became so terrified that one day several hundred of them stopped a supply train, swarmed aboard it, and fled from the camp. Work on the railway stopped completely.

One afternoon, not long after the workers had deserted the camp, the lions were spotted in the bush. That night Patterson took up his watch on a shaky, wooden platform supported by four

poles, with the carcass of a donkey below him as bait. For a long time everything was quiet; then Patterson heard a twig snap and the rustling of a large body creeping through the bush. He soon realized that the lion was stalking him, and paying no attention to the donkey. For almost two hours the beast edged closer and closer to the shaky platform. If it should spring up at him and break one of the poles, he would have almost no chance. Then the lion stopped still, and Patterson could just see it crouching among the undergrowth. He raised his rifle, aimed carefully, and fired. The mighty roaring and groans which followed told him that his shot had been true.

One man-eater was dead, but there was still another to terrorize the camp. Once Patterson managed to wound it, but it escaped into the bush. After a few days it attacked again. The next night, Patterson, perched high in a tree, watched over the tent where the beast had last visited. As he had hoped, the lion came back for another easy meal, and Patterson shot it. But he did not kill it, and the lion limped away into the bush. The next morning Patterson tracked it down and shot it dead.

The good news spread, and the labourers poured back into camp. Work on the line, which had been brought to a stand-still for three weeks by the man-eaters, started cheerfully again.

Patterson shoots the lion

34 THE KINGDOM OF BUGANDA

IN CHAPTER 32 we read how the Arabs of Zanzibar wanted ivory and slaves so much that they started sending caravan parties into the interior of Africa to trade with the African chiefs. The word 'caravan' has a rather different meaning from our modern meaning. It meant a company, usually of merchants or pilgrims, travelling together. The Arab caravans usually consisted of perhaps a dozen Arabs and some 200 African porters carrying on their heads their supplies and the goods with which they traded — cloth, beads, rolls of wire, and guns. They journeyed inland from the coast along well-beaten trails, and gradually they went further and further. By about 1840 caravans were reaching the region of the Great Lakes (see Chapter 38) and finding their way northwards, round the west of Lake Victoria, some years before any Europeans had ever seen these lakes.

North of Lake Victoria is a country called Buganda, which has good soil and regular rainfall. When the Arabs reached there, about 1844, they found a prosperous state governed by a ruler called the Kabaka. Its chief town was near where

Mutesa's capital, with his palace and court on the top of the hill. From a drawing by H. M. Stanley in 1878

Kampala, the modern capital of Uganda, now stands. The first people to invade Buganda were not Negroes, but probably came from Ethiopia; then dark-skinned people from the Nile Valley (see Chapter 4) moved southwards. These mixed with the Bantu Africans and became one people.

By the time the Arabs arrived, Buganda was strong and powerful. The Kabaka lived in a fine palace, surrounded by his officials, wives, and slaves. He appointed officials to rule different parts of his kingdom, but he kept strict control over them, making them report to him at his court every year so that he should know just what was happening.

The people of Buganda mainly grew bananas, and they made a kind of flour by drying and grinding up bananas. They pounded up the bark of certain trees until it was quite soft, and they made cloth out of it. The women did most of the farming, while the men built large canoes, both for trading and for fighting. The men spent much of their time training as soldiers and fighting wars.

In 1862 the first Englishman, John Speke, to explore this part of Africa reached Buganda. In Book 2 of this series there is the story of how Speke found the source of the river Nile. At this time the Kabaka of Buganda was called Mutesa the First. Speke stayed with him for 6 months, and he wrote this account of his first meeting with Mutesa. 'We came in sight of the king's palace. It was a magnificent sight. A whole hill was covered with gigantic huts, such as I had never seen in Africa before . . . The mighty king was reported to be sitting on his throne in the state hut of the third tier. I advanced, hat in hand . . . The king, a good-looking, well-figured, tall, young man of 25, was sitting on a red blanket spread upon a square platform of royal grass.'

Mutesa the First had come to the throne a few years before. He had started his reign, as many tribal kings did, by putting to death any rivals to the throne. Then, as soon as he was secure on the throne, he began to make his kingdom strong. He improved the training and discipline of his army and also their weapons. Most of the soldiers

Modern Buganda women wearing their national dress

fought with spears or bows and arrows, but Mutesa had as many as a thousand armed with guns, bought from the Arab traders. Then, with this powerful army he raided his neighbours on all sides. He did not want to take their land, but he wanted to make them so afraid of him they would never dare attack him. Altogether he carried out about sixty of these raids. He captured their cattle and ivory, and also a great many men, women, and children, whom he sold as slaves to the Arabs.

Mutesa believed that the Arabs and other foreigners brought wealth to his country, and so he welcomed them. He allowed the Arabs to build mosques and, later, he allowed Europeans to send Christian missionaries, though he himself never became either a Moslem or a Christian. He died in 1884. About 16 years later the Kabaka of Buganda made an agreement with Britain, and his country became part of the British Empire. Today, Buganda is part of the independent republic of Uganda.

35 THE HYENAS AND THEIR MEDICINE-MAN

The Hyenas' meeting

ONCE UPON A TIME the hyenas were sitting round the bones of a dead zebra in a rocky valley and holding an important business meeting. They took turns to get up and speak, and after every speech there was polite clapping and grunts of approval. But most of them were not really listening, for they were each trying to decide which of the zebra bones would have the best meat on it. No one hurried, and the speeches were very formal, for the hyenas, as they sneaked through the shadows round a village at night, had seen that this was the way in which men handled business matters.

Then a very old and wise hyena stood up. He was greatly respected, and all the others paid attention. 'I think we need a medicine-man,' he said. 'We don't get enough good advice these days. Now if we only had someone who could tell us about the future, and knew something about magic, and could explain our dreams and cure our illnesses, things would be much better. Man is an ugly creature and no friend of ours, but in practical affairs I must admit he is very successful. Surely this is all because he has medicine-men to work for him.'

The Great Ground Hornbill

All the hyenas howled in agreement, and began to discuss whom they should ask to be their medicine-man. At last they decided to invite the Great Ground Hornbill; so they sent a very young hyena to find him.

The Great Ground Hornbill is a big, stupid bird, as large as a turkey, almost too big to fly. Most of his body is black, but he has a bare, red neck, and as he waddles through the bush you can hear him grunting, 'Ooomp, ooomp.'

Hornbill came to the meeting and said that he would be delighted to serve as Chief Medicine-Man to the Hyenas. Then he began to wonder what they wanted him to do, and at last he thought of a rather clever question: 'Ah-ooomp!' he said, 'Ah-ooomp! Which of my many jobs do you want me to do first?'

At once there was a lot of shouting. 'Tell us where to get food!' screamed one or two. 'Magic! We must have magic!' howled others. One said, 'I had a strange dream last night,' and another, 'What will happen next week? That's what I want to know!'

'Oh dear!' said Hornbill to himself. 'I must do something. I don't know any magic nor anything about dreams. I have enough trouble finding

76

food for myself. Perhaps the safest thing would be to foretell a little of the future for them.' He cleared his throat and said, 'Ah-ooomp! Kindly listen to me. I hope you will be pleased with what I have to reveal. In the future there will be no more day. I have arranged this for you because you hyenas like to hunt by night. The moon will appear as usual; but daylight is finished!'

'Hurrah!' shouted the hyenas. 'Now we can raid Man's villages and eat his animals without having to stop when daylight comes!' They started making plans to raid a village that very night. Meanwhile Hornbill wandered off to look for insects in the grass.

All the hyenas set off just after dark, thinking greedily of the tasty goats and donkeys they would soon kill. When they reached the village after midnight, everything was quiet, and all the people were asleep. They killed two donkeys and nearly a dozen goats and settled down to eat them. As they feasted, they chuckled and grunted and screamed with pleasure, and some of the villagers, awakened by the noise, stirred in their beds. 'The hyenas are very busy tonight in the rubbish pit,' they said.

The feast went on all night long, for Hornbill had told them the night would last forever, so the hyenas were not worried about being caught at daybreak. Then, when they were all beginning to feel comfortably full, the sun rose in the east. The astonished hyenas abandoned their meal and fled in panic towards home. One old hyena who couldn't keep up hid himself in a heap of reeds.

When the villagers came out of their houses and saw the dead animals, they were furious. They soon found the old hyena hiding in the reeds and speared him. Then they all set off after the rest. When they caught them in the rocky valley, they killed many of them, and only a few hyenas escaped into the hills.

Several weeks later, the hyenas gathered sadly again in their valley. First they sent for their medicine-man to find out what went wrong. But Hornbill sent a message saying he was sorry but he had other business. So they dismissed him from his post, and discussed whom to have as their next medicine-man. After much discussion, they decided to invite the Francolin, a shy, little black and brown bird, who runs swiftly through the grass and keeps out of people's way.

This time the hyenas chose wisely. The Francolin accepted their invitation, and he has been the hyenas' medicine-man ever since. When it is getting dark, if you listen very carefully, you will hear his high-pitched, soft cry: 'Ki-i-kit! Ki-i-kit!' He is telling the hyenas to come out from their rocks and hunt. In the early morning, when it is not yet light, he whistles again, long before any other bird, telling the hyenas that they should go home.

But the hyenas have never forgiven the Great Ground Hornbill, and if they see him waddling alone in the long grass, looking for fat insects, they chase him away.

The Francolin

The Hyenas attack the village

36 A GAME PARK

Wildebeeste and Zebras

IF YOU WANT TO SEE WILD ANIMALS, there is hardly any part of the world better to go to than some parts of Africa. In old days, when there were fewer people in Africa and they had only spears or bows and arrows, there were always plenty of animals on the grasslands and in the forests. But when men had guns and greedy traders wanted more elephant tusks and ostrich feathers and sportsmen wanted big game shooting, the big animals were becoming scarce. In fact, some, such as the okapi, a small giraffe-like animal, almost vanished. But now people are realizing that they must protect their wild animals. In most African countries today there are national parks or big game reserves where no one is allowed to kill the animals and where we can see them living in their natural surroundings. One of the largest of these is the Kruger National Park in the Transvaal in South Africa, which covers 8,000 square miles. Here we are describing a visit to the Mara game reserve in Kenya.

The party set off by car from Nairobi at 9 a.m. one October morning. Instead of taking tents and camping at one of the camping sites in the park, as people often do when they go 'on safari' (a Swahili word meaning journey), this party meant to stay in comfort at Keekorok Lodge.

They drove first on the main tarmac road to the north, then westwards along a very rough dusty road to Narok, where they had to sign the askari's (policeman's) book at the check-post by the Uaso Nyiro river. They were amused to see a gathering of Masai warriors, very smart with fresh red ochre plastered on their hair and bodies, skin purses hanging round their necks, sandals made out of old tyres, and spears in their hands. Probably there was to be a dance in Narok later that day (see Chapter 39).

The party, after picnicking on the grass in the shade of thorn-trees, drove on another 50 miles across the grassy plains to Keekorok. On the way they saw wildebeeste, a few ostriches, a family of warthogs trotting along one after the other, great numbers of gazelles, three groups of giraffes, and at one point a herd of about 150 zebras.

Keekorok Lodge, which they reached about 3.15 p.m., consisted of a main building of local stone with a cedar shingle roof and a number of bungalows with stone bases and log walls. The bungalows, each containing two or three rooms,

A Cheetah

Ostriches

bathrooms, and a verandah, were arranged in a semicircle on a grass mound, overlooking a stream and away to the Tanzanian hills. They smelled pleasantly of cedar wood.

After tea, a Masai guide called Simeon, dressed in khaki shirt and shorts and a black beret, with bead bracelets on each wrist, took charge of the party. He spoke Swahili, which one of the party was able to translate. First they looked for lions, for which Mara is famous. After driving about a mile down a grassy track, they came to an outcrop of grey stone, on which lay two lionesses with three month-old cubs playing round them. A little way round the rock lay two splendid maned lions. Every now and then one of them would sit up or roll over contentedly on his back. They looked well-fed and sleepy, and they paid not the slightest attention to the car-full of visitors.

As Simeon led the party back by another route, they passed a lone buffalo, looking rather bad-tempered, three elephants, and some water-buck. Simeon explained that at this time of year (October) the hills of the Mara are teeming with wild animals, but by January many of them will be on the move south to the Serengeti game park in Tanzania.

The next morning, by 6.30 a.m., the party were ready to start again with Simeon. The air was noisy with bird-song, and a distant zebra was barking. They headed north-west, but after half-a-mile the way was blocked by five big elephants and a baby. The car made a detour across the plain and soon met eight buffaloes, which swerved away into thick bush. The next excitement was a pair of ostriches with four babies, which a jackal was trying to attack. The chicks trotted along with their mother, while the father flapped his wings and struck out with his powerful legs whenever the jackal made an attack. At last the jackal gave up, at any rate for the moment.

On the way back, the party were lucky enough to see a fine old male rhinoceros lying on the open plain, with a female and baby sleeping beside him. When they went out again in the evening, they spent some 20 minutes watching a lioness feeding and playing with her two 3-week-old cubs near a stream-bed. On the way home they saw a magnificent cheetah sitting alone on the hillside.

The next morning, after another short expedition before breakfast, the party made the long drive back to Nairobi.

Giraffes

37 THE MOUNTAINS OF EAST AFRICA

Kilimanjaro

EVEN THOUGH THEY ARE NEAR TO or even on the Equator, some of the East African mountains are covered with snow all the year round. This is because they are high — Mount Kenya, which is on the Equator, is over 17,000 feet high. Therefore, though the lowlands are very hot, the air near the summit of the mountain is too cold for the snow to melt.

The highest mountain in Africa is Kilimanjaro, which is on the frontier between Tanzania and Kenya. It is a huge, dome-shaped mass which rises nearly 20,000 feet out of a hot, dry plain.

Like most of the mountains of eastern Africa, it was once a volcano, and it still has a crater at the top, which is several miles round. You can climb down into the crater over the snow and find caves of ice in the walls of rock.

Mount Kenya is perhaps the most beautiful. It is about 100 miles north of Nairobi, the big city of Kenya, and on a clear morning you can see it easily from the city. The country of Kenya is named after its mountain; the word 'Kenya' is only a shortened form of 'Kirinyaga', which is what the people of that part of Kenya call the mountain. These people, the Kikuyu, used to believe that their God lived on the top of Kirinyaga.

Across the Equator in the far west of Uganda lie the Mountains of the Moon, which the local people call the Ruwenzori. They are a long range of mountains, not so high as Kilimanjaro and Mount Kenya, which run between Lake Albert and Lake Edward and separate Uganda from the Congo. Their tops are nearly always hidden in rain and mist.

If you were to climb any of the East African peaks you would find that you passed through much the same kind of country, with the same trees and plants, on each one. All of them have

The Ruwenzori or Mountains of the Moon

Mount Kenya. The plants in the foreground are giant lobelias and giant groundsel

fields and farmland round the base, and all the high ones have bare rock, ice, and snow at the top. Between the base and the summit you pass through belts of tree and plant life which change as you get higher.

To climb Mount Kenya, for example, this is what you would do. You probably start from the pleasant little country town of Nyeri. You have to prepare carefully with the proper food, medicines, sleeping bags, compass, maps, and so on, for mountain climbing is dangerous if you have not got the right equipment. You start very early in the morning in a Land-Rover and drive for some 20 miles through the farming country of the Kikuyu. The land gradually rises until the edge of the forest comes in sight. There is a sharp dividing line between the farms and the forest, which rises at the edge of the farmland like a great green wall. You drive into the forest by the rough track the foresters use for bringing out timber. The branches of the trees often meet over the track, making a tunnel, and the cedar and podo and olive trees grow very tall. So it is rather dark and quiet. At about 9,000 feet high the track passes into a forest of bamboo, where there is nothing to be seen but the straight, yellow stems and feathery, green leaves of the bamboos. And then at about 10,000 feet you come out into open moorland.

This is as far as you can go by car, for much of the moorland is swampy, and the dry part is rough and full of tussocks. Most people make a camp here and stay for a while in order to get used to the height. If you try to climb too quickly you will suffer from mountain sickness, for at this height the air is thin and does not have enough oxygen in it. The moorland has some very strange plants, such as the giant groundsel, a tall, untidy plant, the woody stems of which make good firewood, and the beautiful giant lobelia which holds water cupped in its great leaves. You then walk steadily uphill across the moorland until you come to the top hut at the upper end of the moorland, where you will camp again. Above this there is nothing but slopes of scree (loose stones) and glaciers and walls of rock, with no plants at all, stretching up to the summit. You start from the hut in the early morning to avoid the mists which often form later in the day, and it is not hard to reach Point Lenana, which is 16,300 feet high. But the final pyramid of the mountain, headed by its twin peaks, is steep and difficult, and only experienced rock climbers can reach the very top.

38 THE RIFT VALLEY AND THE GREAT LAKES

Fishing boats on Lake Victoria

FROM THE NORTH TO THE SOUTH of East Africa there runs a valley which is like a huge trough in the earth's surface. In some places it is 100 miles or so wide; in others as little as 20 miles. It varies, also, in depth: where the rift valley runs through mountainous country, even the bottom of the valley is several thousand feet above sea-level; but the bottom of Lake Tanganyika is more than 2000 feet below sea-level. This great crack in the earth's surface, which originally made the Rift Valley, really starts in Turkey; it forms the valley of the river Jordan and the Dead Sea, runs under the Red Sea, and splits the mountains of Ethiopia into two parts. The great lakes of Rudolf, Tanganyika, Malawi, and many others have formed in the valley, which finally runs through Mozambique to the sea. The valley divides as it crosses East Africa, and Lake Victoria lies in the country between the two parts.

Lake Victoria is the biggest of the lakes — in fact, it is bigger than any other freshwater lake in the world except Lake Superior in North America. It is like a great inland sea. When sailing across it, you are out of sight of land for several hours on end. Kenya, Uganda, and Tanzania, whose frontiers meet in the middle of it, all have ports on Lake Victoria, from which steamers carry passengers and cargo across it. Great storms with very high winds often build up over the lake, making big waves, and when a storm is coming, all the many fishing boats run for shelter.

The Equator runs through the north of the lake, and so the climate is always warm, but this part of East Africa is in high country, and Lake Victoria is nearly 4000 feet above sea level, higher than any part of the British Isles except the top of Ben Nevis. Therefore the climate is not uncomfortably hot. Most of the people living round the lake are fishermen, and they also have small farms growing maize or bananas and vegetables. They live in villages of thatched huts, and though there are many different tribes, they all live in much the same way. Many of them fish in small dug-out canoes, but today there are also bigger motor-driven boats with more modern fishing tackle. The fishermen go out in the evening a mile or so from the shore and let down their nets in long lines held by floats. They leave them all night and come back the next morning to collect the catch. Those fish they eat themselves, they cut up and dry in the sun. They send a great deal to the towns to be sold in the markets or to freezing factories who pack it and send it to the cities of East Africa. The fish they usually sell is called tilapia, and it is very good to eat.

Lake Tanganyika is long and narrow and in places very deep. Its western shore belongs to the Congo and the eastern shore to Tanzania; in the north is the little state of Burundi, and the south reaches into Zambia. Lake Malawi is mainly in Malawi, though Tanzania and Mozambique have part of the eastern shore.

In some parts of the Rift Valley smaller lakes have formed with no rivers running out of them. They lose moisture only through evaporation in the hot sun, and so, as the years pass, they have collected more and more sodium salts which do not evaporate in the sun. By now there is so much sodium that animals cannot drink the water, nor fish live in it. But tiny plants called algae grow very well in it, and these are good food for any animals who can manage to eat them without drinking the poisonous water. Flamingoes can do this. With their enormous curved beaks they skim the slimy, greenish surface of the water, and they twist their long necks so that the water runs out through a sort of filter in their mouths, and the algae plant-food goes down their throats.

Lake Nakuru in Kenya is one of the best places to see flamingoes. Hundreds of thousands of them can be seen feeding along the marshy shores, making the lake appear as though it were edged with a strip of bright pink. If they are disturbed, they rise in a mass of whirring wings, their bodies gleaming red, pink, and white in the sun. Lake Natron in Tanzania, which lies far away from inhabited country, is the main place where flamingoes breed. In a great expanse of marsh and mud in the middle of the lake the birds make nests on the top of mounds of mud, and rear their babies safe from enemies. About half the flamingoes in the world breed on Lake Natron and live on the soda lakes of the Rift Valley.

Flamingoes on Lake Nakuru

39 THE MASAI

A Masai manyatta (camp)

THE MOST FAMOUS FIGHTERS in East Africa in the days before the white men came were a people called the Masai. They lived on the wide plains in southern Kenya and northern Tanzania, down the Rift Valley, and across to Lake Victoria. They used to raid their neighbours on every side and steal their cattle, and all the neighbouring tribes feared them because of their skill in war. The Kikuyu people, who lived in the wooded country to the east, left a long strip of forest uncut as a protection against Masai raids, and part of this forest barrier is now Nairobi City Park.

The Masai are a handsome people, tall and slim, with fairly light brown skins, straight noses, and hair that is usually worn long. They are only partly Negro: they are mostly of the same race as the ancient Egyptians. In fact, the people of southern ancient Egypt probably looked quite like the Masai of today.

The Masai live in a very beautiful part of Africa. It consists of miles and miles of rolling grassland, dotted with thorn-trees, and broken here and there by a rocky hill or a lake or the crater of an old volcano. The people move about according to the season, seeking the best grazing for their herds; and so they make no permanent houses or villages. When they settle in a place for a while they build a kind of camp, called a manyatta, where a group of families lives for a few weeks or months at a time. Then they move on, taking their few belongings with them and burning the old manyatta to the ground.

To make a hut, they plant a framework of wooden stakes in the earth; then they bend these over in a series of hoops. They next fill in the framework with leaves and twigs and mud, and plaster the whole of the outside with cow dung, which quickly hardens in the sun. They leave an opening for the door, but there are no windows or shutters. A whole hut is only about 5 feet high, so that grown men cannot stand upright inside. There is no furniture, except perhaps a little stool for the head of the family.

They arrange their huts in a big circle, and around the outside of the circle, they build a

Masai women and children

thorn fence, about 7 feet high and with several openings, where people and their animals can go in and out. In the evenings the village herd is driven inside the enclosure, and the openings are barred. Then all the people and animals of the manyatta are safe from any wild animals which may be prowling outside.

When they are young, Masai children have a very free life in the open air. They wear nothing except a few strings of beads; but as they grow older, the boys wear little tunics of cloth, and the girls, leather skirts with bead embroidery. They seldom go to school, even now, because most of their parents are not interested in the modern world, and schooling does not fit in with their wandering life. Instead, the children receive instruction from the elders in the customs and history of the tribe, and they are trained in the skills they will need when they grow up.

The girls help their mothers to collect firewood and make the cooking-fires. They carry water from the nearest spring, and collect the family's milk in long, decorated gourds. They learn to sew beads on to leather for belts and skirts, and they make ornaments for their arms and legs by winding coils of copper wire round them. Sometimes they walk with their mothers to the nearest trading-centre to buy sugar and matches, maize and vegetables. But even when they grow up and are married, the girls do not have to work very hard for their families, for much of the hardest work of hut-making and load-carrying is done by the older women.

Boys start learning to be herdsmen and warriors when they are very young. At 7 or 8 they begin to milk the goats and cows, and go out with their fathers to herd the animals. Before they are in their teens they must be able to manage a herd alone. They learn from the warriors how to throw spears and wield swords, and they practice with dummy weapons made of wood. When they are about 15 or 16, they are made full warriors of the tribe at a solemn ceremony, and for 10 years or more, they leave their family homes and live with all the other warriors of their age-group in a special village.

During these years of military training, the young men have no possessions and are not allowed to marry. They live on a diet of milk and of blood taken from the necks of living cows. They no longer cut their hair, but roll it into long plaits plastered with fat and red clay. They wear nothing but a red cloth tunic draped over one shoulder, a leather purse on a string round the neck, and ornaments. Nowadays, when there are no tribal wars and they are forbidden to raid their neighbours' cattle, the warriors have little to do. Their chief excitement is hunting. A Masai lion-hunt is a great test of courage, and the warrior who first spears the lion is greatly honoured and receives the mane as his prize.

Masai warriors

After their military service, the young men become first senior warriors and then elders. They can marry and settle down to a life of ease, herding cattle and discussing village affairs with the other older men. Some Masai elders nowadays are beginning to plan changes in the old ways. Already they are breeding better cattle, and building dams to store water, and asking here and there for schools to be started. Since the Masai are rich and intelligent, they will make swift progress once they accept the ways of the modern world.

40 A KIKUYU VILLAGE IN KENYA

THE KIKUYU PEOPLE are the largest tribe in Kenya. They live in the central part of the country south of Mount Kenya, and their land is high, fertile, and well-watered. Hardly any of it is flat. It consists mainly of dozens of long ridges, with deep valleys between them. In the valleys there are small, swift-running streams which carry the rain that falls on the mountains down to the Athi and Tana rivers, and so out into the Indian Ocean.

The village of Kahama stands on one of these ridges in Nyeri District, which is the north part of Kikuyuland. To get to it from Nairobi you drive out northwards for nearly 90 miles along the main tarmac road to Nyeri, and then, before reaching the town, you turn off left along a dirt road. Climbing all the way up the ridge for about 15 miles, you come to Kahama, which is about 7,000 feet above sea level. You can see the edge of

household carrying is still done on people's backs, especially women's backs. You see women trudging home under great loads of firewood, the straps that hold the wood on their backs passing round their foreheads. Here and there women and girls are bringing up drums of drinking water to their houses from the streams in the valleys. All of them are wearing European-type dresses in bright colours.

Kahama is a small trading-centre, with little stone-built, tin-roofed shops arranged round an open market square. Most of the shops are general stores, selling maize, millet, beans, sugar, and honey, and cooking-oil, charcoal, and paraffin. There is a petrol filling-station, a carpenter, a cobbler, and a second-hand clothes shop. There is also a co-operative office and a health centre. A church stands on a little hill to one side, and as you

A Kikuyu market day

the forest a mile or two beyond, and the peaks of the Aberdare Mountains rising above the trees. There is not much traffic once you leave the main road — a few cars and lorries, an occasional bus, and Government Land Rovers with the names of their offices painted on the driver's door. There may be one or two donkey-carts, but most of the

enter the village you see a thatched primary school with mud walls. At the far end of the village, standing in its own grounds, is a big day secondary school which is built all of stone. There are several stone houses for the teachers, some of whom are English and American. Otherwise, the houses in the village are round, thatched huts, and most of the people who live in them are either workers in the village or farm-workers who do not have land of their own.

Farm land is very precious here; it comes right up to the outskirts of the village. The farms themselves are mostly small, the average size being only about 7 or 8 acres: a few farms are much bigger than this, but even a big one is only about 50 or 60 acres. Many of the men go away to work in Nairobi, or on big estates elsewhere, and leave their land to be worked by their wives and families. The full-time modern farmers, who own the bigger farms, often lease more land from their neighbours, whenever they can.

Mr. Solomon Kamau is one of the bigger farmers, and he has studied at the local Farmers' Training Centre. He runs a good modern farm employing several workers. His 35 acres are just along the ridge from Kahama, and he rents another 10 acres from a neighbour as grazing land for his herd of Guernsey cattle. All his land is well fenced into fields and paddocks, and near the house there are pig-sties, a chicken-run, a milking-shed, and a dairy. The house itself is quite new — a comfortable, L-shaped house of several rooms built of stone with a corrugated-iron roof and a chimney. Most of his neighbours' houses are the same shape, but many are built more cheaply of wood with walls of plastered mud. Mr. Kamau's old mother prefers an old-fashioned, round hut with a grass roof, and this she has at the end of Mr. Kamau's garden.

A good variety of crops is grown on the farm. There are enough vegetables to feed the family throughout the year and leave some over for selling in the Saturday market in the village.

Mr. Kamau's farm

Some of the fields are planted with maize and others with beans. Mr. Kamau usually grows maize in a field for two years at a time, then beans for one year. Then he plants the field with grass as pasture for the cattle for three years. This gives the field a rest, and also the cattle help to fertilize it. Mr. Kamau also grows a little pyrethrum — a white daisy from which insecticides are made. But his main cash crop is tea, of which he has four acres and is planting more. He sends the tea-leaf by bicycle every day to a collecting-point in Kahama, and from there lorries take it to the new tea factory a few miles away. For this he gets cash for buying the things he needs for the farm.

Mr. Kamau and others like him are making some of this Kikuyu country more productive than it has ever been before. They work hard, and their district is beginning to look rich and well cared for. They are proud of the progress their country is now making, and glad that they can send their sons to secondary schools and that there are good opportunities for the future.

41 A SOMALI ENCAMPMENT

Somalis making an encampment

THE SOMALIS, who live in the Horn of Africa, south-east of Ethiopia, are a tall, slim people with black, wavy hair, brown skins, and usually fine features. There are many different tribes, and as a whole they feel far more loyal to their family clans and their tribes than they do to their country. They have been influenced a good deal by people coming from Arabia, and they follow the Moslem religion. Also in the south they have married with Negroes. Somalis are, most of the time, a cheerful, easy-going people, courteous and hospitable to strangers; but they are quick to anger, and once they have started a feud with anyone — another family or tribe, or with people of another race — they are slow to forgive, and the feud may last for many years.

Somalia is a hard country to live in for, although there are some fertile river valleys, a great deal of the country is hot desert or poor, sandy and rocky grassland, and there is never enough water. Some of the tribes, especially those who are partly Negro, have settled near the two main rivers in southern Somalia and are farmers. They grow rather poor crops of beans and maize and a kind of grain called *dura,* but they have a hard time as the rivers dry up almost completely for a large part of the year.

The majority of the Somalis despise farming and are herdsmen, moving about from place to place in search of grass for their animals. Some of them keep cattle or goats, others keep camels. The camel-owners are the proudest, and they look down on the cattle-men and despise the farmers as slaves. For more than 500 years the Somali herdsmen have been on the search for better grazing land and have always been moving outwards from their homeland, driving other people away. They now live in parts of northern Kenya and over the border into eastern Ethiopia, as well as in Somalia. Still today a Somali tribe will trespass on to other people's regular grazing lands and try to take their water, and then fierce fighting will break out. This happens especially across the Ethiopian frontier, where there are constant battles and bloodshed, for the Somalis and the Ethiopians have been enemies for centuries.

Anyone travelling by Land Rover along the rough, stony tracks which are the 'roads' of northern Kenya, southern Ethiopia, and Somalia, may well see as evening comes on a clan of Somali herdsmen building their encampment. It takes them very little time. Having tethered the camels, they unload from their backs bundles of curved sticks and rolls of skins and mats. The boys and girls hurry off with knives to cut branches from the stunted thorn trees growing round about; with these they make a strong fence round the encampment to keep out wild animals such as leopards during the night. The older boys, meanwhile, plant the curved sticks in circles in the ground, making dome-shaped frameworks for the huts. These are then covered with the mats and skins, making groups of round huts rather like beehives. The women may make a fire, but they do very little cooking. The food they like best is milk, usually curdled, which they get from their herds — camels, cattle, or goats. They have a rough corn bread, and perhaps also some vegetables. When they do eat meat, which is seldom, they usually prefer it uncooked.

The encampments are made, where possible, in places where there is a waterhole, probably dug in a dry river-bed, and these may be 20 or 30 miles apart. When the huts are made, the men start bringing up water from the well, for which as many as eight men may be needed. The men stand on cross-beams or in alcoves in the walls of the well. The man at the bottom fills a leather bucket and passes it to the man above, and so on to the top. Each man passes full buckets up with his right hand and empty ones down with his left, and a steady flow of water pours into the clay troughs at the well head. The older children get the big herd of thirsty camels or cattle in order, and move them up, a few at a time, to drink at the troughs. It is a busy scene, noisy with the singing of the men in the well and the cries of the thirsty animals.

Life has changed very little in Somalia over the years. Since the country became independent of Britain and Italy in 1960, other countries have tried to help the people to farm better and to build schools and hospitals. But it is almost impossible to make people pay taxes when they are always on the move, and the Somalis pay very little attention to laws. Even their language is hardly written down, though they have a great many songs and folk-tales passed on by word of mouth.

Somali men drawing water from a well, while their cattle are drinking

42 LOCUSTS IN THE HORN OF AFRICA

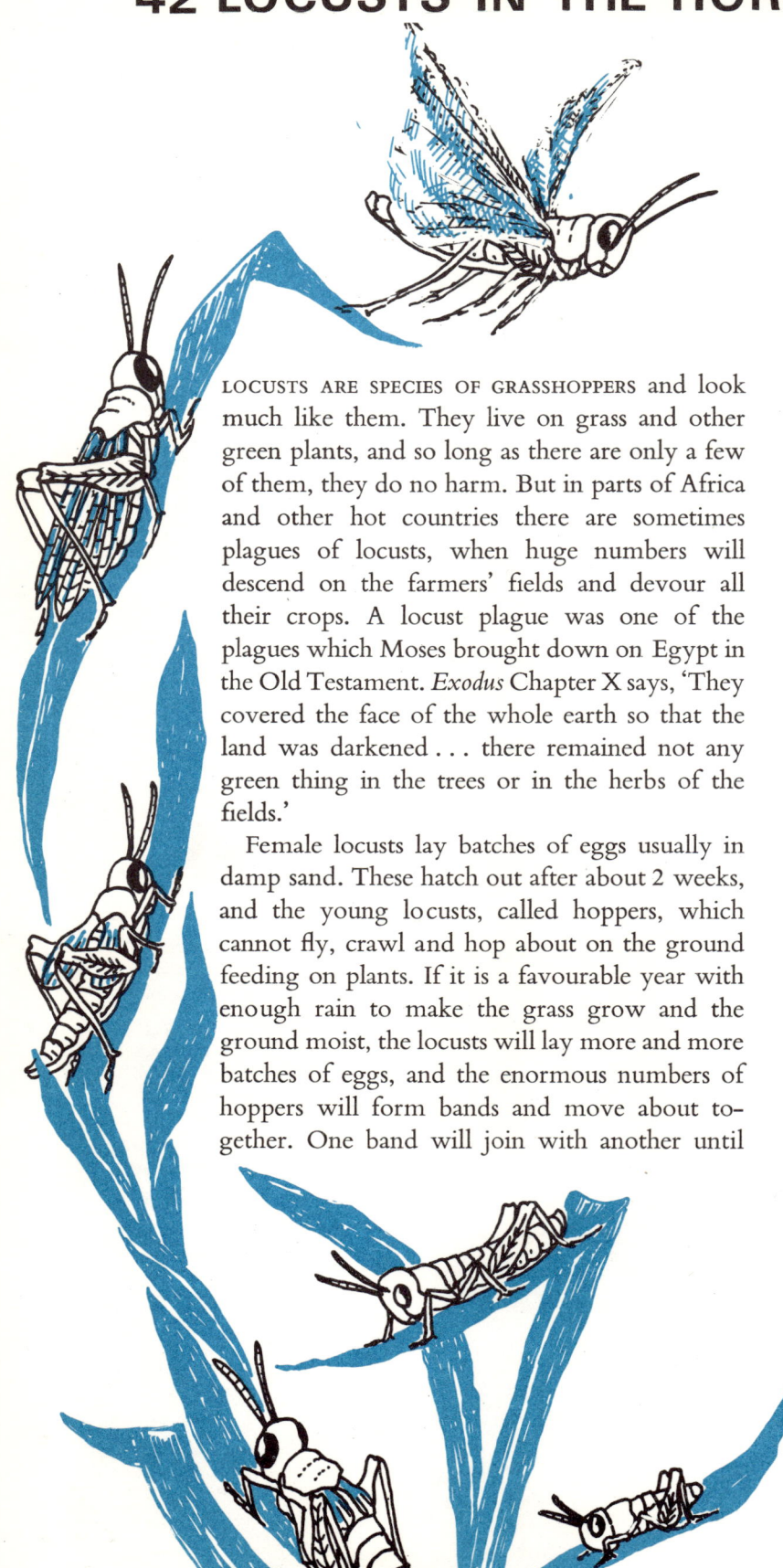

LOCUSTS ARE SPECIES OF GRASSHOPPERS and look much like them. They live on grass and other green plants, and so long as there are only a few of them, they do no harm. But in parts of Africa and other hot countries there are sometimes plagues of locusts, when huge numbers will descend on the farmers' fields and devour all their crops. A locust plague was one of the plagues which Moses brought down on Egypt in the Old Testament. *Exodus* Chapter X says, 'They covered the face of the whole earth so that the land was darkened... there remained not any green thing in the trees or in the herbs of the fields.'

Female locusts lay batches of eggs usually in damp sand. These hatch out after about 2 weeks, and the young locusts, called hoppers, which cannot fly, crawl and hop about on the ground feeding on plants. If it is a favourable year with enough rain to make the grass grow and the ground moist, the locusts will lay more and more batches of eggs, and the enormous numbers of hoppers will form bands and move about together. One band will join with another until there are many thousands in a group, which strip the land of every green leaf.

When, after 4 or 5 weeks, the locusts are fully grown, they have developed wings and can fly. So, as soon as food begins to grow short, the whole band will rise in a great closely-packed swarm and fly to fresh grasslands. At first they make quite short flights, settling on new ground and feeding through the night. But as more and more hoppers become fully grown and the swarms grow larger, they migrate much greater distances, perhaps several hundred miles if the wind is behind them. By then a swarm may contain many million locusts, and when they fly they look like a great threatening cloud, blotting out the sun, and, as the Old Testament says, darkening the land. These terrifying swarms bring disaster to the place where they settle. They strip the land of every green growing plant, and flatten the bushes and break branches off trees by the weight of their numbers. When they fly off again they leave a brown and devastated wilderness behind them. Even when the plants begin to grow again, new swarms of younger generations follow up behind and devour these.

There are some animals, particularly storks, which eat the locusts, and they have a good time when there are plagues of locusts. And there are some human beings who find locusts good food. The Bible tells us that when John the Baptist went into the wilderness to pray, taking no food with him, his meat was 'locusts and honey'.

Today, scientists have found out how to control these terrible locust swarms. At first people tried laying down poisoned bait in the places where the young hoppers hatch. This killed many insects, but it was very expensive and difficult to carry out, and also it was wasteful for it killed a great many animals and birds as well. Another method is to spray the swarms with insecticides from low-flying aircraft. It is important to attack the swarms while they are still small and before

they have done much damage, and far better to destroy them while they are still hoppers and have not been able to breed.

Now that scientists know much more about the life history of locusts, they can tell much better where and when locusts are likely to increase in numbers. There is an organization called the Desert Locust Control Organization, which has its headquarters in Asmara in Ethiopia. All the countries which are likely to suffer from locust plagues contribute money to this, and the Organization sends scouts out to watch for the beginnings of swarms, and local people report to the Organization when they see signs of trouble. As soon as a breeding swarm is found, aircraft are sent to attack it before it grows big. In these ways, this terrible plague has been largely stopped in north-east Africa; but the success of the Desert Locust Control Organization depends on the various countries co-operating with each other. Were they to quarrel, the locust plagues would soon be back.

The farmer and his wife are banging tins to try to drive the locust swarm away, an emergency method which is often successful

This time it did not succeed. The locusts have eaten every leaf

43 ETHIOPIA

Ethiopians going to market across the mountains

IN CHAPTER 6 WE READ how the great trading city of Axum grew up in the cool highlands of northern Ethiopia, and lasted until about the 7th century. Now, we have travelled all round Africa, seeing what Africa used to be like in the past and what it is like today, until we have come back again to Ethiopia. We read how, about 330 A.D., Ousanes, king of Axum, became a Christian. Although Axum fell into ruins and is now no more than a village, Ethiopia still remained a Christian country, and the kingdom of Ethiopia is one of the oldest still surviving kingdoms of the world.

Ethiopia is a rather strange country, different from anywhere else and always rather cut off from the rest of the world. This is largely because it is so high and mountainous that it is not easily reached from outside. Round its borders to the north, west, and south the land falls steeply away to deserts below, and to the east the land falls sharply to the Red Sea. Inland, the high lands are cut by deep, rocky gorges through which the rivers run. So it is not an easy country in which to build roads or railways. It is surrounded by countries who follow the Moslem religion, and who have looked on it as an enemy because it was Christian. In the 19th century when Europeans divided up almost all Africa between them (see Chapter 26), Ethiopia still remained independent. She has always been independent except for 5 years, from 1936 to 1941, when the country was conquered and occupied by Mussolini's soldiers from Italy.

The Emperor of Ethiopia has his royal palace in the hilly city of Addis Ababa, nearly 9,000 feet above sea level. The Ethiopians call their Emperor the King of Kings, or sometimes the Lion of Judah. This reminds us of the legend that he is descended from King Solomon of Judah and the Queen of Sheba. The people living in the centre of Ethiopia, which we used to call Abyssinia, are the Amharas, who for a long time have been the ruling people, and their language, Amharic, is the official language of the country. It is written in a special alphabet of its own. But there are many other peoples in the country, speaking different languages. Some of them are closely related to the Somalis, others have mixed with Negroes in the past. These different peoples had their own tribal kings, and usually paid more attention to them than to the Emperor.

Towards the end of the 19th century, a strong and wise man, Menelik II, became Emperor. He not only united the country, but brought in many foreign experts to help him run his government, and invited a French company to build Ethiopia's first railway, from the coast up to Addis Ababa. His good work was carried on when Haile Selassie became Emperor in 1930. He built roads, hospitals, and schools, and even started a university. He set up a proper system of taxation, and kept a firm control over the local chiefs. But although he brought in many European ideas, he never forgot that Ethiopia is an African country, and he is doing all he can to help the African countries to work together — over such matters, for example, as controlling swarms of locusts (see Chapter 42).

A modern church at Axum

Ethiopia is still, according to our ideas, a very backward country. Far the greater number of people still cannot read or write, and even today most of the farmers plough their fields with wooden ploughs drawn by oxen, sow their seed broadcast, cut the grain with sickles, and thresh it by treading it out and winnowing it in the wind. Most people live in small villages of thatched, mud-walled, round houses, clustered round a church. The towns are usually little more than market places, where the buildings have corrugated-iron roofs. Most of the transport is still by mule, donkey, or pack-horse, for though the main towns are now joined by made roads, over most of the country there are nothing but tracks. Many people hardly leave their homes, except to go to the local market.

All the same the soil is fertile, the country not overcrowded, and the people are well-fed. They grow a small grain called *teff*, out of which they make round, flat, unleavened loaves, which they eat with a hot, peppery sauce called *wot*. They brew a kind of beer called *talla*, and also make an intoxicating drink from honey, called *tej*. They eat some meat, but keep beef for special occasions, when they often eat it raw. As a whole, they are still very contented with their lives.

But things are changing. More and more people, as in the rest of Africa, are demanding schools for their children, doctors and hospitals for their sick, and better roads and transport. The Ethiopians have been lucky in having a wise Emperor who long ago decided that they should have these things, not by violent revolutions, but through hard work and steady progress.

An Epiphany procession to a church cut out of the rock face, at Lalibela

INDEX

Aberdare Mountains, East Africa, 86
Abyssinia, *see* Ethiopia
Accra, capital of Ghana, 41
Achimota, college in Ghana, 41
Addis Ababa, capital of Ethiopia, 92
Afrikaans (language of Afrikaners), 51
African Lily-trotter (bird), 20
African peoples, 12: Baganda, 74; Bantu, 75; Barotse, 64; Bushmen, 46; Fan (or Fang), 36; Hottentots, 12; Kikuyu, 86, 80, 84; Masai, 84, 78; Matabele, 53, 62; Pygmies, 12, 46; Rozwi, 63; Somali, 88; Wolof, 38; Zulu, 48
Afrikaners, European people of Dutch origin in South Africa, 51, 52
Aggrey, Dr. James, West African educationalist, 40
Albert, Lake, 14, 80
Ali bin al-Hasan, early ruler of Kilwa, 69
Amharas, people of Ethiopia, 92
Amharic, language of Ethiopia, 92
Angola, Portuguese colony in West Africa, 58
antelopes, 46, 65
apartheid, policy of racial separation, 57
Arabian settlement in Zanzibar, 70
Arabs, Bedouin, wandering desert people, 23
askari (policeman in East Africa), 78
Askia the Great, 15th-16th century ruler of Timbuktu, 27
Asmara, city in Ethiopia, 91
assegai, short Zulu spear, 48
Atlas Mountains, 11, 23
Axum, ancient kingdom of Ethiopia, 18, 17, 92

Bamako, capital of Mali, 27
Bantu, a group of African peoples, 75
baobab, tropical tree, 39
Barotse, tribe of central Africa, 64
Benin, ancient kingdom of West Africa, 29
Berbers (desert people), 23
birds (African), 20
black ivory (slaves), 70
Blue Nile, tributary of Nile, 14
Boer War (1899–1902), 51
Boers, people of Dutch origin in South Africa, 52
British South Africa Company, 52
Buganda, country of East Africa, 74
Burundi, country of East Africa, 83
Bushman rice (termites' eggs), 47
Bushmen (of Kalahari Desert), 46, 12
Bussa Rapids, on Niger, 29

cacao, cocoa tree, 42
Cairo, capital of Egypt, 14
Cam, Diego, Portuguese captain, 32
Cameroons, *map*, 10
Cape Colony, province of South Africa, 52
Cape Coloured, a people of Cape Province, 55
Cape of Good Hope, 11, 50, 58, 63

Cape Town, South Africa, 50, 11
Caravan: in desert, 26; in East Africa, 71, 74
caravan routes, 26, 23
Chaka, Zulu chief, 48
cheetah, African animal, 78
Christianity: brought by Portuguese, 32; European Missions, 58; in Ethiopia, 92
cocoa farming, in Ghana, 42
coconuts, in Zanzibar, 70
Congo: ancient kingdom, 33; European colonization, 59; slave trade, 70
Congo, river of West Africa, 36; *map*, 11
crafts: in Benin, 29; Bushmen, 47; in Kush, 17; Masai, 85
crocodile, 30, 64
crops of Africa, 12: cocoa, 42; coconuts, 70; fruit, 56; groundnuts, 38; maize, 33, 83, 87; millet, 33, 39; tea, 87

Dakar, capital of Senegal, 38
dams: Kariba, 65; Lake Kyle, 62; Niger, 28
Dar es Salaam, capital of Tanzania, 68
Dark Continent (Africa), 8
Da Gama, Vasco, Portuguese explorer, 10
De Beers Mining Company (diamonds), 52
desert: Sahara, 22; Kalahari, 46
Desert Locust Control Organization, 91
dhow, Arab sailing boat, 68, 64
Diaz, Bartholomew, Portuguese discoverer, 10
Dingaan, Zulu, brother of Chaka, 49
Dingiswayo, African chief in Natal, 48
drum language, 45
dura, Somali grain, 88

Egypt, country of north-east Africa, 14, 90
elephants, 79, 64, 30
Ethiopia, country of north-east Africa, 92, 18, 59, 88, 91
Ethiopia, emperors of, 92, 18

Fan (or Fang), tribe of the Congo, 36
Farmers' Training Centre, Kenya, 87
farming: in Africa, 9; in Kenya, 87; in Somalia, 88; in Ethiopia, 93; in South Africa (fruit), 54
Fez, city in Morocco, 26
fishing: in Lake Victoria, 83; in Senegal, 39; in the Zambesi, 64
flamingoes, birds of East Africa, 83
folktales of Africa: "The Hare and the Pumpkins" (Malawi), 66; "The Hyenas and their Medicine-Man" (East Africa), 76; "The Tug of War" (probably West Africa), 30
Fort Victoria, town in Rhodesia, 62
francolin, African bird, 77
fruit, in South Africa, 54

Gabon, 36
Game Reserves, 78

Ghana: ancient kingdom, 24; modern Ghana, 41, 42, 58
giraffes, 78
gold: mining: (The Rand), 56; (The Transvaal), 51; trade: in ancient Axum, 18; in ancient Ghana, 24; in Zimbabwe, 62; in West Africa, 33; in Kilwa, 68
Great Trek, 50
Ground Hornbill, African bird, 76
groundnuts, African crop, 38, 29
Guinea, country of West Africa, 10; Gulf of, 29

Haile Selassie, Emperor of Ethiopia, 93
Henry, Prince of Portugal, 32
hippopotamuses, 64
honey-guide (bird), 20
hoppers (young locusts), 90
Horn of Africa, 88, 10
Hottentots, African people, 12
houses: in ancient Ghana, 25; in Ethiopia, 93; in Kenya, 86, Masai, 84; in Senegal, 38
hunting: by Bushmen, 46; for elephants, 70; for lions, 85
hyenas, 76

irrigation: Nile Valley, 14; Transvaal, 54; Rhodesia, 62
Isis, Egyptian goddess, wife of Osiris, 14
Islam (Moslem religion), 23, 88, 92
ivory, *see* trade

Jameson, Dr. L. S., 53
Johannesburg, South Africa, 56, 51; *map*, 11

Kabaka, ruler of Buganda, 74
Kalahari Desert, South Africa, 46; *map*, 11
Kampala, capital of Uganda, 75
Kariba Dam, 65
Kenya, country of East Africa, 86, 68, 83, 89
Kenya (Kirinyaga), mountain of East Africa, 80
Khartoum, capital of Sudan, 24
Kikuyu, tribe of Kenya, 86, 80, 84
Kilwa, ancient trading city of Tanzania, 68
Kilimanjaro, highest mountain in Africa, 80
Kimberley, diamond-mining centre, Orange Free State, 52
Kingsley, Mary, traveller in West Africa, 36
kraal, Zulu village, 49
Kruger National Park, the Transvaal, 78
Kruger, Paul, President of the Transvaal, 51
Kush, ancient kingdom of the Upper Nile, 16

Lake Kyle Dam, 62
Lakes, of Africa, 82; *map*, 11
Lander, Richard, British explorer, 29
Limpopo river, South Africa, 52; *map*, 11
Lion of Judah (title of Emperor of Ethiopia), 92
lions, 72, 79
Liberia, first Negro Republic, 59
Livingstone, David, medical missionary and explorer, 64, 58, 70
Locusts, in North-East Africa, 90

Malawi, country of Central Africa, 82, 66
Mali, country of West Africa, 10, 26
Manicongo, 15th-century King of Congo, 33
Mansa Musa, 14th-century Emperor of Mali, 26
manyatta, Masai camp, 84
Mara Game Reserve, Kenya, 78
Marabou Stork, 21
Masai, people of East Africa, 84, 78
Matabele, tribe of Rhodesia, 53, 62
medicine-man (witch-doctor, magician), 76
Menelik II, Emperor of Ethiopia, 92
Meröe, capital of Kush, 17
military training, tribal: in Buganda, 75; Masai, 85; Zulu, 49
missionaries, 58, 75
Mohammed, Moslem prophet, 26
Mombasa, town in Kenya, 68, 72
Monomatapa, King of Zimbabwe, 62
monsoon winds, 68
Morocco, country of north Africa, 27
Mosioa-tunya (Smoke Thunders), African name for Victoria Falls, 65
Moslem, *see* Islam
mosque, Moslem place of worship, 69, 75
Mountains of the Moon (Ruwenzori), Uganda, 80
mouse-bird, African bird, 30
Mozambique, country of East Africa, 82
mummy, preserved body, 15
Mungo Park, Scottish explorer, 28
Mutesa, ruler of Buganda, 75

Nairobi, capital of Kenya, 87, 78; City Park, 84
Napata, capital of Kush, 16
Narok, town in Kenya, 78
Natal, province of South Africa, 48
national park (game reserve), 78
navigating by stars (in desert), 23
Negroes, *see* African peoples
Niger, river of West Africa, 28; *map*, 11
Nigeria, country of West Africa, 58
Nile, river of Egypt, 14
Nubia, *see* Kush
Nyeri, District and town in Kenya, 86, 81

oasis, fertile place in desert, 23
Obas, kings of Benin, 29
oil, in Sahara, 23
Orange Free State, province of South Africa, 52, 50
Orange River, South Africa, 50; *map*, 11
Osiris, Egyptian god, 14
ostrich, 20, 78
Ousanes, King of Axum, 19, 92

Park, Mungo, Scottish explorer, 28
Patterson, Lt. Col. J. H., railway engineer, 72
Pharaoh, king of Egypt, 15
podo, East African tree, 81
Portuguese exploration of West Africa, 32, 64
Pygmies, African people, 12, 46
pyramid, tomb of Egyptian kings, 15

railways: in Ethiopia, 93; in Uganda, 72
Rand, the, *see* Witwatersrand
Red Sea, 92, 82
Renders, Adam, discoverer of Zimbabwe, 62
rhinoceros, 79
Rhodes, Cecil, colonial pioneer, 52
Rhodesia, country in central Africa, 52
Riebeeck, Jan van, Dutch colonist, 50
Rift Valley, East Africa, 82, 9, 10
Rissik, Johannes, after whom Johannesburg is named, 56
Rozwi, people of Zimbabwe, 63
Rudolf, lake, 82
Ruwenzori (Mountains of the Moon), 80

sacrifice, human, 29
safari, Swahili word for journey, 78
Sahara Desert, 22, 26, 10
Salisbury, capital of Rhodesia, 62
sandstorm, 23
savanna, tropical grassland, 60
'Scramble for Africa', 59
secretary bird, 21
Selous, F. C., hunter in east and central Africa, 62
Senghor, Leopold, President of Senegal, 38
Senegal, country of West Africa, 38, 58
Serengeti, game park in Tanzania, 79
Seth, Egyptian god, brother of Osiris, 14
Sheikh (Arab tribal leader), 23
shifting cultivation, form of farming, 10
Sheba, Queen of, 18, 92
slavery: West Africa, 34; East Africa, 70; markets, Arab, 70
sleeping sickness, 60
snake-bird (African Darter), 20
Solomon, King of Israel, 18, 92
Somali, north-eastern African people, 88, 92
Somalia, country in East Africa, 88
Speke, John, English explorer, 75
Stanley, Henry, explorer of Africa, 44
storks, 90
Sudan (country of black men), 24
Swahili, language of East Africa, 68

Table Mountain, Cape of Good Hope, 50, 53
talking drums, 44
Tanganyika, *see* Tanzania; Lake, 14

Tanzania, country of East Africa, 68, 71, 83
terrace farming, 19
Tete, trading settlement on the Zambesi, 64
Timbuktu (Mali), 26
Touaregs, desert tribe, 27
trade: in ivory and slaves, 70, 64; in Axum, 18; in Buganda, 74; European, 58; in ancient Ghana, 24; in Kenya, 86; in Kilwa, 68; in Timbuktu, 26
Transvaal, the, province of South Africa, 53, 50
"Travels in West Africa", book by Mary Kingsley, 36
trypanosomes, germs of sleeping sickness, 60
Tsavo, river of Kenya, 72
tsetse flies, 60

Uganda, country of East Africa, 70, 75, 72, 83
Uitlanders (foreigners), gold miners, 51
universities: Timbuktu, 26; Ethiopia, 93

Victoria Falls, Zambezi, 65
Victoria, Lake, 10, 74, 82
volcanoes, East Africa, 80, 84
Voortrekkers, 50

wadi, desert river valley, 22
water, drawing of, 14, 89
weaver (bird), 21
White Nile, *see* Nile
Wilberforce, William, Englishman, opposed slave trade, 35
wild animals: in game reserve, 78; lions, man-eating, 72; on the Zambezi, 64; birds, 20; in folk-tales, 30, 66, 76
wine making, in South Africa, 55
witch-doctor, *see* medicine-man
Witwatersrand (Ridge of White Waters), 56
Wolof, tribe of Senegal, 38
writing, discovery of by Egypt, 9

Zambezi, East African river, 64, 52
Zambia, country of central Africa, 52, 83
Zanzibar, island off East African coast, 70
zebra, 79, 46
Zimbabwe, ancient African city, 62
Zulu, tribe of Natal, 48

ACKNOWLEDGEMENTS

The author wishes to make acknowledgement to J. F. Carrington, whose book *Talking Drums of Africa* provided much of the information for Chapter 19. Also he wishes to thank Geraldine Elliot for the story *The Hare and the Pumpkins,* which appears in *The Long Grass Whispers,* and H. T. Harman for the story *The Hyenas' Medicine-man,* which appears in *Tales Told Near a Crocodile.* He wishes also to acknowledge indebtedness to John G. Williams, from whose book *Birds of Africa,* published by Collins, the material for Chapter 7 has been taken.